Who Holds `

THE RETIREMENT VAULT

A Guide to Protecting Your Assets in an Age of Uncertainty

BY
JOSEPH A. LEONARD

Industry Consultant

SECOND RIVER
HEALTHCARE PRESS

Who Holds Your Combination to The Retirement Vault
A Guide to Protecting Your Assets in an Age of Uncertainty

By Joseph A. Leonard

Second River Healthcare Press
26 C Shawnee Way
Bozeman, MT 59715

Phone (406) 586-8775
FAX (406) 586-5672

Editor: Michelle Nash
Cover Design: Mark Bond

Leonard, Joseph Who Holds Your Combination to The Retirement Vault / Joseph A. Leonard

ISBN-10: 0-9814605-0-X (hard cover) ISBN-10: 0-9814605-1-8 (soft cover)
ISBN-13: 978-0-9814605-0-5 (hard cover) ISBN-13: 978-0-9814605-1-2 (soft cover)

1. Retirement & Estate Planning 2. Elder Care 3. Retirement Investments

I. Leonard, Joseph II. Title

Library of Congress Control Number: 2008921988

First Printing May 2008

Disclaimer: While every precaution has been taken in preparation of this book, the publisher and author assume no responsibility for errors or omissions. Neither is any liability assumed for damages resulting, or alleged to result, directly or indirectly from the use of the information contained herein. If you do not wish to be bound by the above, you may return this book with receipt to the publisher for a full refund.

AUTHOR'S NOTE

This book addresses important estate planning issues for individuals and families. Although intended to provide an introduction to the legal, tax, investment and financial planning for your estate, you should not consider it your sole source of information and advice for these topics. Each case may be different, and laws, or the interpretation of laws, may change. The recommendations provided are general in nature and may not be suitable for everyone. This book should never be considered a substitute for the advice of a qualified professional. When seeking professional services, consult with businesses or individuals that are dedicated to a specific field. An estate planner or elder care professional should take each case on individually, as each family's plans are unique and should receive personal attention.

I would like to thank many people for their contributions to this book. I am grateful to my wife Kristi and my children Kamryn, Julianna, and Isabella, for their patience, and allowing me to devote the necessary time to the book. I thank my friend Ken Mostella for all of his knowledge and research, and for handling all of the day-to-day operations with the agents and services we provide. Jeff Wofford, our attorney, deserves my gratitude for his input and review of all of the legal aspects, and continuing education he provided to us—a step ahead of the forthcoming law changes. I am indebted to my Uncle Chuck and Aunt Doe for all their tutelage from the very start of my career, not only in business, but also as role models in life. Finally I would like to thank all of our advisors, Katrina and all our office staff, for their time and input to make this book possible. All of you are the very best.

I hope you enjoy, and benefit from, the years of research and experiences shared in this book.

Joe Leonard

Table of Contents

RESOURCES

Chapter 1 The Who, What, When, Why and How of Estate Planning

"Rule number one: Never lose money.
Rule number two: Never forget rule number one."
- Warren Buffet

Who needs an estate plan? The answer is: Anyone who has a need or responsibility to pass down or protect any form of asset. Essentially, that means EVERYONE. Estate planning gives you the peace of mind of knowing you have done everything to protect your assets. Estate planning will eliminate probate costs, limit or eliminate potential family squabbles, and either eliminate or reduce estate taxes.

What does estate planning involve? Simply put, it is the process of examining what you want to happen with your assets in case of disability, confinement, or death. Nearly all clients are looking to accomplish some of the following through estate planning:

- I always want to be in control if I'm able.
- If I'm not able to make my own decisions, then I want my loved ones to do it for me.
- When I die, all of my assets will be directed to my loved ones according to my instructions.
- Whenever possible, I want to arrange for this to take place without taxes, fees or court costs.

As an advisor to thousands of clients, the four principles that

I adhere to are simple:

1. Asset protection.
2. Steady growth, no up and down fluctuations of investments during retirement.
3. Distributions to heirs according to **your** wishes.
4. Reduce or eliminate risk.

If these statements mirror your estate planning goals, then you are reading the right book. Without a proper estate plan in place, you and your family can lose control over your property. You may possibly suffer unnecessary attorney and court costs and pay excessive taxes. This is all irrelevant if you think you have not paid enough taxes. (I am still looking for that person!) Fortunately, these problems can all be avoided by implementing a proper estate plan that will pass your property on to your loved ones, if that is your wish.

WHAT IS JOINT TENANCY AND SHOULD I AVOID IT?

Joint tenancy is when two or more individuals jointly own or hold title to property and each owner has equal rights to the use of the property in its entirety. The following examples illustrate joint tenancy and some common pitfalls.

- You created joint tenancy with your son on your home and one bank account. When you pass away, your son will legally own these two assets. He has no legal obligation to split these with any of your other children, regardless of what your will or trust may say, since the assets automatically pass outside probate to the joint tenant upon the death of the other tenant. Your children will always do the right thing when you are no longer here, won't they? Even if the child does the right thing, he or she may incur unintended gift taxes.
- If a parent remarries and retitles the family home with the new spouse, the children of the first marriage will

lose all rights to the home if the parent dies before the new spouse. The property will pass automatically to the surviving spouse.

- If an elderly parent puts the family home in joint tenancy with an adult child, the parent loses exclusive control over the home. The parent will not be able to sell or refinance the home without the approval of the child. Also, the parent's home is then exposed to the child's liabilities, such as automobile accidents, bankruptcies, debts and divorce settlements. This can be perilous.
- If a child is named as a joint tenant and the child dies first, the property may be taxed as part of the child's estate. Then when the parent dies, it can be taxed a second time.

WHAT HAPPENS IF YOU DON'T MAKE A PLAN FOR YOUR ESTATE?

When you pass away with no legal instructions as to your estate, you die "intestate." An unpleasant surprise may be in store for your survivors, because the government will fill in the blanks with what they think it should be. After all debts, probate costs, and taxes have been paid, the court will divide the remaining estate according to the laws of intestate succession.

Let me give an example. A client's husband died without a will (intestate). He was married previously and had three children from that marriage. At their father's death, they assumed they would get his assets because he was only married to his second wife for three years. They might have gotten all of his assets had he created an estate plan. But since he did not, state law gave the first $115,000 of his estate to his surviving spouse, plus one-half of the remainder over that amount. The intestate statutes did not take into account those items held jointly with her spouse at his death, such as their home. The second wife ended up with more than 95% of all of the assets because her husband did not plan his estate.

My advice to you is: **PLAN**, **PLAN**, **PLAN**.

CHAPTER 2 WILLS, TRUSTS AND PROBATE

"A crisis is a change either sudden or evolving that results in an urgent problem that must be addressed immediately." **- Source: "Crisis Management" Harvard Business Essentials**

A will is a set of instructions advising the probate court how you want your assets and property divided after your death. It also designates whom you want to represent you as the personal representative or executor of your estate. You may also designate a guardian for any minor children.

The most common type of will is known as a "sweetheart" will. Upon the death of the first spouse, everything is left to the surviving spouse—the sweetheart. If there is no surviving spouse, then everything is divided and distributed among the living children. If there are no living children, the will usually provides for the assets to be distributed to any grandchildren or the living heirs pursuant to state law. If no heirs are found, the state becomes the heir and takes all.

THE PROBATE PROCESS

Probate is the legal process wherein the court oversees the identification and appraisal of all probate property, as well as the distribution of such property pursuant to the will's instructions. The court also ensures that creditors are notified and paid. Usually the court sets a time limit in which a creditor may make a claim against the estate. In most states, that is three or four months. The estate cannot be closed until this time has elapsed and settlement with the creditors has been satisfied. In most cases, you can expect probate to last in excess of one year. Some cases may go on for several years.

Should I Want to Go to Probate?

Many may argue that probate is a good thing because it provides potential heirs, or others who think they have a valid claim against the estate, access to make their claims in open court. It is also argued that the court supervision of probate benefits society by providing an orderly way of deciding a person's estate. These statements may be somewhat true, but read on.

Should I Want to Avoid Probate?

Cost is the first reason why most heirs want to avoid probate. The average cost of probate is between 3% and 8% of the value of an estate. This consists of court costs, inventory fees, attorney fees, personal representative's fees, bonds and accounting fees. This can amount to a lot of expense. If you go to probate without a will, the costs may even be higher. Additionally, if your will is contested, the probate process may take several years to be settled, and the costs will certainly be much greater.

The probate process takes place in open court, where the family's private financial records are made public record. This can be a major issue with some people, and, in many states, this information is now available via the Internet. This also means anyone who thinks there is something to gain can try to make a claim. Remember, there is no privacy in public documents.

Can I Avoid Probate?

Many people tell you to put your children's names on all of your assets to avoid the probate process. This may be true. However, no one ever advises of all the potential unintended consequences of simply putting your children's names on your assets, like those of joint tenancy discussed earlier or potential estate and gift tax.

What Is the Best Way to Avoid Probate?

TRUSTS, TRUSTS, TRUSTS. Using trusts is simply the best and easiest way to bypass probate. One primary function of a trust is to eliminate probate. However, trusts also shorten the time necessary to administer the estate, assure privacy, make it nearly impossible for anyone to successfully contest the estate, and generally are more cost effective than probate. There are many different types of trusts suited to various specific purposes. The following are a few of the most commonly used trusts.

THE REVOCABLE LIVING TRUST

A revocable living trust is probably the most commonly used trust for estate planning purposes. This particular estate planning vehicle works very similar to a corporation. Think of it as the corporation of Mr. and Mrs. Jones. Quite simply, the trust (or corporation) holds title to the assets of Mr. and Mrs. Jones. Mr. and Mrs. Jones are in charge of their trust as the "trustors" and have full reign to do whatever they want with whatever is in the trust. They may use or move any of the monies, property and investments as they see fit. The trust is amendable and revocable, even after the death of the first spouse. Upon the death of the second spouse, the trust becomes irrevocable and the trust assets are distributed pursuant to the trust provisions. You will name your successor trustees, usually one or several of your children. Your successor trustee(s) takes over the management of your trust upon the death of the trustors and is responsible for the distribution of the trust assets as provided within the trust. Because the trust holds title to the property and the successor trustee(s) has the ability to transfer trust property to the beneficiaries without court intervention, probate is avoided. Again, one of the primary functions of this type of trust is to avoid probate.

Many people wrongly believe that if they put all of their assets into a trust, they are protected from long-term care issues. A trust will NOT protect your assets from what is called Medicaid spend-down. If you have access to your money in the trust, then so does Medicaid.

A/B TRUSTS

An A/B trust or credit shelter trust is a more specific type of trust that is created when a couple has an estate subject to the estate tax. Essentially, an A/B trust locks in the applicable exclusion amount of the spouse who dies first, to ensure that the surviving spouse is not taxed on the entire estate.

Here's an example of how it works: Assume that a couple has an estate of $4 million. Without an A/B trust, the entire estate goes to the surviving spouse at the death of the first spouse, since most couples hold their assets jointly. There is no tax problem at that time because of an unlimited estate tax exclusion in transfers between spouses. However, on the death of the second spouse, the entire $4 million estate is subject to the estate tax. The surviving spouse has his or her $2 million applicable exclusion, but the remaining $2 million in the estate is taxable at about 50%, or $1 million of tax. With an A/B trust, the $2 million applicable exclusion is locked in for the spouse who dies first and the remainder goes to the surviving spouse. Then at the death of the second spouse, the first spouse's $2 million applicable exclusion is used. The second spouse's $2 million applicable exclusion is also used and the entire $4 million estate is transferred estate-tax-free. Additional reasons and uses for this type of trust are beyond the scope of this discussion.

IRREVOCABLE TRUSTS AND THEIR PURPOSE

Irrevocable trusts are just that, irrevocable. They provide for the distribution of assets to beneficiaries at fixed intervals and amounts that cannot be altered without court intervention. The value of the trust assets are locked in for estate and gift tax purposes and protected from creditors and/or lawsuits. These types of trusts are used in many contexts. The most common and beneficial is the special needs trust, wherein the trust assets are set aside and locked in for beneficiaries who cannot or may not be able to care for themselves. By creating this type of trust, the special-needs individual will not be disqualified for any governmental assistance otherwise available to him or her. These types of trusts may also be used for a trust beneficiary who is a spendthrift. Assets within an irrevocable trust generally may not be attached by creditors or assigned by the beneficiary, thus ensuring that the beneficiary, and not a creditor, will receive the monies. Needless to say, irrevocable trusts are specialized trusts that are not suitable for everyone. There are many types of irrevocable trusts, most of which are beyond the scope of this discussion.

OTHER TYPES OF TRUSTS

There is an alphabet soup list of other trusts. These include trusts such as irrevocable life insurance trusts (ILIT), grantor retained annuity trusts (GRAT), grantor retained unitrusts (GRUT), charitable remainder annuity trusts (CRAT), and charitable remainder unitrusts (CRUT). These trusts are all highly specialized and are used mostly for sophisticated income and estate tax planning beyond the scope of this discussion.

The content and information in this chapter was provided by Jeffrey L. Wofford, JD, LLM.

Chapter 3 Long-Term Care Insurance

"The 80 plus population is growing five (5) times faster than the general population."
- Source: NBC News, 2000

Long-term care (LTC) insurance, in essence, is a health policy for late in life, designed to pay for nursing home costs. When you consider the aging population, including the Baby Boomers, and that one out of three men over the age of 65 will need long-term care, you can see how long-term care insurance can be vital to the financial future of the elderly and their families. The AARP states that 7 out of 10 people who have reached the age of 75 will require some type of long-term care. However, few Americans plan for these eventualities. Most elderly don't plan on having their children take care of them in their homes, or they may not want that to happen.

Often, the cost of long-term care can exceed an individual's annual income. If steps are not taken to purchase long-term care insurance or other measures to protect your assets from these costs, you may watch as your entire estate is liquidated. Medicare may pay for some of your home healthcare needs and a minimal number of days in a nursing home, but contrary to popular belief, this public health plan doesn't pay for long-term care.

According to Elder Care Online, there are four key issues to compare when considering long-term care or extended care insurance:

- **The benefit period**, which is the length of time that the insurer will pay for care after a claim has been filed. This coverage period can range from one year to a lifetime.
- **The daily benefit**, which is the maximum dollar amount

or percentage amount the insurer will pay for care, each day, during the coverage period. These insurance benefits can range from $30 to hundreds of dollars a day.

- **The elimination period or deductible**, which is the length of time and the amount of money that must be paid out-of-pocket before the insurer starts to pay. This could be a day to a year or even longer.
- **The level of inflation protection**, which is a policy rider meant to cover the amount your benefits will increase over time due to inflation. A hundred dollars today might be adequate, but in 10 years it may be too little. Also you need to know at what percentage the cost of care is rising. In 2004 and 2005, it was approximately 15% to 18%. If your inflationary protection is only 5% per year, it is not going to keep up.

A common question that many people ask today is: What is the likelihood a person will need long-term care? According to AARP, by the year 2020, an estimated 12 million older Americans will need long-term care. Most will be cared for at home; family members and friends are the sole caregivers for 70% of elderly people. A study by the U.S. Department of Health and Human Services indicates that people age 65 face at least a 40% lifetime risk of entering a nursing home. About 10% will stay there five years or longer.

WHAT IS THE COST?

This question mark is the largest reason that most retired Americans do not have long-term care insurance. Through my own experience of asking approximately 10,000 retirees how many carry LTC insurance, the response has been less than 5%. And the number one reason is cost. The average cost for a typical policy for a person 65 years of age is approximately $2,450 per year. For many retirees living on a fixed income, this may be too much of a burden.

A few years ago in a seminar for a group of retirees, I had a gentleman ask me, "So what is considered expensive?" I replied,

"If it hurts you to write that check, then it must be expensive to you." Expense is relative to what you have and the means by which you live. For example: Say you have $1 million in liquid assets, and you're paying $5,000 a year for a good policy for you and your spouse. This may be considered inexpensive. However, if you pay $5,000 per year and you only have $100,000 in liquid assets, this might not be such a good deal.

WILL IT COVER WHAT I NEED WHEN I NEED IT?

After you choose a policy, most companies will offer an inflationary rider. This rider, with most companies, will allow your policy to cover 5% more in costs each year with the hope of keeping up with inflation. The sad part is that the cost of long-term care is rising at a much higher rate than 5%. Let me give you an example: You are 60 years old and purchase this policy:

- Covers $150 per day
- Has a 5% inflationary rider
- The cost to be in a nursing home today is $150 per day

You have adequate coverage for TODAY. However, suppose you don't go into long-term care today, but instead you go in when you are 80 years old, perhaps 20 years down the road. What is the cost of long-term care then? If it continues to rise on the path of 10% to 15% per year, your coverage would cover **less than half** of the cost. This is, of course, assuming the premium you have been paying never goes up. Since that's never going to happen, let's look at the numbers:

Now	**20 years from now**
$150 per day of coverage	$325 per day of coverage
	Actual costs $650 to $700

In this case, it just doesn't add up. You would still be covering more than half of your daily expense while your insurance would be paying the lesser amount. This would cause your estate to dwindle very rapidly.

Another main issue is that policies can change the rate you are paying for your coverage. You may be paying $2,100 per year for your coverage at age 60. However, when you turn 70 your rate may rise to $3,000, and when you turn 80 it may rise once again, this time perhaps up to $6,000 per year.

Are you still on a fixed income? You might be forced to drop the coverage because you can't afford it anymore. That's exactly what the insurance company would love you to do. You just paid in 20 years of premiums and they didn't have to pay out any claims. Insurance companies statistically never lose!

HOW DO I QUALIFY FOR COVERAGE?

LTC insurance is a medically underwritten policy. That means that if you have a pre-existing condition, you may not be eligible for coverage. If you have heart problems, cancer, diabetes, high blood pressure, or any other major medical pre-existing problems, "GOOD LUCK." Even if you can get coverage with a major pre-existing condition, that condition will determine how much you will have to pay for coverage. Your age is another stipulation when you are trying to purchase LTC insurance. Most companies will offer beginning coverage until about age 75, or sometimes even 80. Very few companies will offer this type of coverage after age 80.

Here's a quick story about a "young" lady at one of my seminars who had a question. She said she bought some LTC insurance three years ago when she was 88 years old (remember, most companies won't even sell it to you after 80), and she was not sure she had what she needed. So I asked her how much she was paying annually for the coverage. Her reply was that she was paying $16,000 a year. "Holy Cow," I said. "I'm going to take a guess and say that no matter what your assets are, this is not a good deal." She said, "Oh no, the guy who sold it to me said it was a great deal." Why do you think that is? Easy— the average commission paid to the agent is about 70% of the premium. Can you see who really benefited?

WHAT ARE THE LIMITATIONS OF LONG-TERM CARE INSRUANCE?

Limitations of LTC insurance can be very confusing. These are some questions that must be asked.

- Is there a waiting period?
- When will my coverage start?
- When will it stop?
- How much per day will it cover?
- Does it cover just a percentage of the costs?
- Does it have an inflationary rider?
- Are there any exclusions?
- Is my rate adjustable or is it locked in? If it is locked in, how long does that rate last?
- If it's a lifetime rate, for whose lifetime does it last—mine or the insurance company's?

I'll give you an example of an average policy.

- 90-day waiting period before start of coverage
- Will pay for up to two years of care with a maximum $150,000 paid out
- Covers $150 per day room and board only
- 5% inflationary rider

If you end up in a nursing home with this coverage, it would work like this. After three months the policy would start to pay up to $150 per day, until you have reached $150,000 or two years. During the second year of coverage, the policy would cover 5% more per day than the previous year.

Chapter 4 Financial Power of Attorney and Medical Power of Attorney

A **financial power of attorney**, also known as **durable power of attorney**, is a legal document wherein another individual or agent is granted the authority to act for another who is unavailable or unable to act because of incapacity due to illness or a lack of competence. When someone has a durable power of attorney or is an agent of another, he or she is able to enter into contracts, negotiate and settle matters as if he/she were that other person.

If an individual becomes incapacitated to the point of being unable to take care of financial matters and does not have a valid power of attorney, family or loved ones must go to court to obtain the legal authority to act on the person's behalf as conservator. Becoming someone's conservator can be expensive and can limit planning opportunities since the court oversees all financial transactions of the conservator.

Let me give you a real example: A client of mine is an only child. Her mother became incapacitated due to dementia. She thought she was O.K. since her mother's assets were modest and her name was on all of her mother's accounts. My client did not have a durable power of attorney for her mother. When her mother had to go to a nursing home, my client believed that she would be able to qualify her mother for governmental assistance due to her modest financial resources. However, when moving her mother out of her apartment, she found a stock certificate in her mother's name for 26 shares of Dayton Hudson stock her mother had purchased while working for the store in 1951. Those 26 shares of stock had become more than 4,000 shares of Target stock worth about $30 per share, or $120,000. Needless to say, my client's mother was not able to qualify for assistance due to the existence of this stock. Further, my client had to become her mother's conservator in order to liquidate the stock to pay for her mother's nursing home care, costing my client nearly $2,000 of court costs, bond fees and attorney fees. Also, since the court was involved, all $120,000 had to be used to pay for the nursing home instead of using certain planning techniques, which would have saved about $80,000 of the $120,000 from the nursing home.

Medical Power of Attorney

A **medical power of attorney**, also known as a **durable power of attorney for health care**, is critical because it allows a trusted agent to make healthcare decisions on your behalf when you are unable because of incapacity from illness or a lack of competence. It allows you or your agent, and not the hospital, to control your medical decisions.

The medical power of attorney helps your doctors determine when life-supporting measures should be stopped. If you wish that life-sustaining measures not be performed in certain circumstances, the agent you name will follow your wishes.

Hospitals and doctors do not want to take on this responsibility. Most everyone followed the tragedy concerning Terry Shaivo in Florida where her family was fighting with her spouse to keep her alive after being in a persistent vegetative state for more than 17 years. Regardless of your view, the reason this became national news was because Terry Shaivo did not have a medical power of attorney outlining her wishes should she become unable to make her own medical decisions. If she had created a medical power of attorney, her wishes would have been followed, rather than her husband's or her family's.

The content and information in this chapter was written by Jeffrey L Wofford, JD, LLM.

Chapter 5 Crisis Management "Post Planning"

"I'll just wait until something happens, and then I'll get help if I need it."

- Many Retirees

The quote shows of one of the most common ways retirees plan (or don't plan) for their long-term care needs and their financial futures. This is also how many elder law attorneys make a living—helping people do "crisis planning."

In February 2006, President Bush signed the Deficit Reduction Act, which included many new laws concerning this very matter. What this did was take away almost every post-planning option that existed before. Trying to circumvent the system is no longer an option and will put more than 80% of Americans in the same situation – unprepared for the 19-plus years they may face in retirement. *Pre-planning almost always works, and post-planning never works.* Think about that.

Many people wait until they have a long-term care issue to seek out someone who will (for a fee) help them protect some, if not all, of their remaining money. The government changed the law making it illegal to do so. It would be like owning a new car and having an accident, then going to your insurance agent and saying, "I now need to get insurance to pay for my accident." They would laugh you right out of their office.

THE MOST IMPORTANT THING IS PRE-PLANNING!

What steps should you be taking to avoid crisis planning? The following are some suggested steps for avoiding crisis planning in the future:

1. Everyone should have a will or a trust for the purpose of directing his or her assets.
2. Have both financial and medical powers of attorney.
3. Have a plan in place for long-term care needs (i.e., LTC insurance or repositioning of your assets).
4. Let loved ones know where to find your important information and the names of people who helped you put this information together.

Of greater concern is that people work all their lives and plan every step of the way.

They plan whom they marry, where to live, how many children to have and what career to pursue. Then they retire and say, "I've made it and now I don't have to do anything." However, this is the most critical time in their life to be planning.

Planning is an ongoing process that should be reviewed at least annualy. Do you realize that most retired Americans spend hours, if not days or weeks, planning their yearly vacations, and then spend less than two hours per year reviewing and planning their retirement portfolios? This is the attitude of the society we live in. Perhaps you plan a little more than the average American, but think of your kids or even your grandkids. How much time do they spend on considering their future?

The biggest crisis we face in the next 50 years, in my opinion, is the lack of planning concerning money. Our generation is a generation of savers, your children are a generation of spenders, and your grandchildren are a generation of borrowers—spending what they don't even have.

Chapter 6 Medicare and Medicaid—What are they?

"The average person can expect to live 19 or more years in retirement."
- Source: Employee Benefit Research Institute

Living well into your retirement years means that you will incur costs for maintaining your health. You should know about Medicare and Medicaid, understanding what they are and what they aren't.

Medicare is a federal benefit that accrues according to your lifelong earnings the same way Social Security benefits accrue. For every year you work, your eligibility increases. If you are not eligible through your earnings history, you can purchase Medicare insurance as long as you are within the age requirements. Medicare is your federal government health insurance program that begins when you reach age 65, or when you are entitled to Social Security disability benefits. You have paid for it all your life through taxation, and it is your primary care health insurance. If you are retired, you still continue to pay a premium for Medicare. Even if you have no immediate plans to use Medicare coverage, it is a good idea to enroll and become part of the system as soon as you are eligible so that you have the paperwork out of the way and can access benefits immediately should you need them.

Typically, Medicare covers 80% of your bills for doctors' office visits, hospitalization, medical equipment, and so on. Medicare does not cover the cost of annual physical exams, most dental care or hearing aids. You may still purchase a Medicare supplement, often known as a Medigap policy. Medicare supplements cover what

Medicare does not. The problem with Medicare is knowing what it covers, especially if you end up in long-term care.

Coverage

Medicare has very strict rules and regulations about what types of care it covers and how much it pays. Medicare determines how much your doctor is paid for the treatment you receive. If a doctor accepts Medicare patients, he or she cannot charge you more for treatment than Medicare will pay. It can be difficult to find participating providers for seniors in some rural areas. There are many things Medicare does not cover, including:

- extended nursing home stays,
- glasses,
- hearing aids,
- checkups,
- private nursing care,
- dental care.

WHAT DOES MEDICARE COVER FOR LONG–TERM CARE?

If you end up in a nursing home or long-term care, Medicare covers the first 20 days at 100%. From the 21st to the 100th day, Medicare covers everything over the federally mandated co-pay. As of this writing, your co-pay portion would be $120 a day. Medicare will only cover everything over that $120 a day. If you have a Medicare supplement, or Medigap policies C, D, E, F, or G, your Medicare supplement policy will cover that co-pay. The importance of having a Medicare supplement in conjunction with the standard Medicare Part A is that it can save you up to $94,000 in co-pay dollars if you end up in a nursing home or in long-term care. After the 100th day, Medicare is finished: It runs out on the 100th day. There is a 100-day cumulative lifetime benefit, not just 100 days each time you go in or out of long-term care. After that 100th day, you now have three choices: First, you pay if you have the money. Second, if you have long-term care insurance, it may cover your expenses, depending on its limitations. Third, you may qualify for Medicaid, but Medicaid will only pay when it considers you to be destitute.

MEDICAID—WHAT IS IT?

Medicaid is a government-funded entitlement program designed to provide health care to people of all ages who meet state and federal impoverishment guidelines. Many people assume that Medicaid will pay for their long-term care. Since they have Medicare, they believe when it stops at 100 days, Medicaid will take over even if they have not exhausted all of their funds. This is not necessarily true. Most people believe Medicaid is welfare. Although a portion of Medicaid goes toward welfare, it is actually intended to help people when money is not there or when the money is in an exempt asset.

How does that work? Medicaid will not pay for your long-term care until you are qualified, which means that you have spent all of your money or non-exempt assets. As of this writing, you are allowed to keep a maximum of $2,000 if you are a single person, and a maximum of approximately $102,000 per couple if you are married.

How do you qualify? Medicaid is a tax-based program that you have paid into for your entire working life. It is designed to assist Medicare when funds are not available. This means everyone is eligible to qualify; however, if you were smart enough to save your own money, Medicaid will require you to spend yours first.

We all know this is not a fair tax-based system. That is why our legislators create loopholes. Most people may wonder for whom they create those loopholes, since the law is the same for everyone. A common saying is, "The rich get all the benefits." That is not true; the rich just know how to use the laws. Loopholes are designed for everyone, but you have to know about them and how to take advantage of them.

Medicaid has established two different lists to qualify you for Medicaid coverage—non-exempt assets and exempt assets. Non-exempt assets are those that can disqualify you. However, Medicaid allows exempt assets. These assets are outlined following:

Non-exempt Assets

- Savings, checking, CDs, and money market accounts
- Stocks, bonds and mutual funds
- IRAs/401(k)s that can be cashed in
- Life insurance above $1,500 face value
- Vacation homes, boats, planes, etc.
- Investment real estate or vacant land
- Brokerage accounts
- Promissory notes not repaid
- Assets transferred within 60 months
- Annuities (not actuarially sound)

Exempt Assets

- Primary residence up to a value of $500,000
- Income-producing property
- Retirement funds in payment
- Personal property/belongings
- One automobile or boat
- Burial contracts and burial plots
- Life insurance up to $1,500 face value
- Current wedding and engagement rings
- Annuities (actuarially sound)

Non-Exempt Assets

Cash assets of any kind are non-exempt, such as cash, savings accounts, checking accounts, money market accounts, and CDs (certificates of disappointment!). As of now, CDs are no longer at 8, 9, or 10 percent interest, as they used to be. High interest rates like that are a thing of the past. It is more like 2 to 3 percent in today's market. Next are stocks, bonds and mutual funds. Also included are your IRAs, 401(k)s, 403(b)s, or any type of brokerage account that can be cashed in. Any asset you may cash out can be used by Medicaid as an asset against you.

Life insurance with a face value of $1,500 or above may have to be sold to pay for your care. You did not buy life insurance to cash it in to pay nursing home expenses, but Medicaid will require you to use that as an asset. The value of vacant property that does not produce an income, a second home, another piece of property, woods, a farm field, or another lot you may own can be used as an asset against you.

Promissory notes that have not been repaid are also considered non-exempt assets. Medicaid will ask if you have loaned any money to your children. They consider a promissory note a loan, so you have to make sure, if it was not a true promissory note that you expect to be repaid, you tell them that it was a gift, which was transferred more than 60 months ago. Medicaid considers any asset transferred within 60 months to be your asset.

Annuities that are not actuarially sound or Medicaid-friendly do not comply with Social Security's life expectancy table and are non-exempt assets. If you have a regular annuity purchased through your broker or from your employer, it is probably not actuarially sound. Approximately 99% of the annuities purchased today are not actuarially sound and are therefore considered non-exempt.

Exempt Assets

Your primary residence is an exempt asset. As of this writing, Michigan and Texas are the only states where your home is still a protected asset. Medicaid cannot attach your home or put a lien on it if you end up in long-term care. That will most likely change very soon, since the Federal Government wants to have the state recovery act established in every state. Then, if you end up in a nursing home and are single or the last surviving spouse to pass away, Medicaid will put a first lien on your home to repay or recover all the money they have paid out in expenses for your care. In some states, including Florida, if you have a letter saying you are in a nursing home, and your home is being used by your child or a dependent under the age of 25, they cannot put a lien on the home. Some stipulations must be met in that case.

Income-producing property is also a complex area. The non-exempt assets include vacant property that is not producing income. If you have a second home or piece of property not producing income and you end up in a nursing home situation, you may rent out that property. If it produces income, it is an exempt asset. However, you cannot rent out that property for $1 to your children. Currently, it has to be rented for 6% of the property value per year. For example, if you have a $100,000 second home, you have to rent it for $6,000 per year. The children may have to consider if they want to keep the asset, or if they want to keep the income they would receive in rent on that asset. It is unlikely that you would be in a nursing home for four or five years, so it is much more important to keep the asset than to sell it.

Retirement funds in payment are another exempt asset. This is your pension. It seems like a protected item, but there is a catch. Medicaid cannot take your pension; it can only take what your pension pays you every month. For example, if you had a pension with $100,000 that was paying you $1,000 a month, Medicaid could not cash out your entire $100,000. It could only take the $1,000 that you are receiving every month.

HOW DO I QUALIFY FOR MEDICAID, AND WHERE DO I GO TO APPLY?

In order to qualify for Medicaid, you should have all your assets in order before you go to the Department of Human Services, formally known as the Department of Social Services. When you go to the Department of Human Services to qualify, you will talk with someone from Medicaid about long-term care. The Medicaid representative will ask you a list of questions to assess your non-exempt and your exempt assets. Your answers to those questions will determine whether they qualify you or not.

Many people mistakenly believe the Medicaid office should be there to help you, since it is a tax-based service that we all pay for. However, technically, their job is to make you spend ***your*** money, rather than spending the tax dollars you paid in. For that reason, it is in your best interest to know how to answer their questions correctly. Each Medicaid qualifier you come in contact with is different. Medicaid, issued at the federal level, is administered by your county or state to assist Medicare when funds are not available.

Tips for handling a Medicaid Hearing or Appeal

- Dress formally in business attire.
- Bring an attorney or qualified planner if possible.
- Bring a family member or friend for support.
- Bring all of your medical records with you.
- Speak calmly and politely.
- Be patient and wait your turn.
- Obtain copies of all documents that are issued at or after the hearing.
- Do not hesitate to have things explained, repeated or read back to you.

Examples:

The following are a few experiences I have had with clients trying to qualify a loved one for Medicaid. In one case, I met with a lady whose husband was in a nursing home, and she went to qualify him for Medicaid. She had put most of her money in certain types of annuities. Her assets were protected for herself, and she had spent her husband's assets down to under $2,000, so everything looked fairly good. Then the qualifier asked a question about her checking account, which showed that more than 10 years ago she wrote checks out to her son and daughter for $10,000 each. The qualifier asked if she loaned any money to her children. Since it was ten years ago, she assumed it was O.K. to answer this question. She said she had loaned them each $10,000 as a down payment on their homes. The qualifier raised his eyebrows and asked when they were going to repay the loan.

Medicaid can assess those loans against her, because she said they were loans. If she had said she gave each child $10,000 as a gift more than 10 years ago, then it would have been acceptable. Any asset that you have transferred more than 60 months ago is

O.K., and Medicaid cannot use that against you. However, if it was a promissory note or a loan, then Medicaid can consider it a non-exempt asset. In this case, they counted the $20,000 she gave away as a loan to be repaid, because she said "loan" not "gift." We all know that money given to your children more than 10 years ago is probably not going to be repaid, but Medicaid would not look at it that way. Remember that any assets that you have given away—whether they are cash, stocks, bonds, mutual funds, property, or anything else of value—are still considered your assets for a minimum of 60 months according to Medicaid. If you have a trust document and your assets are within a trust, they are considered your assets for a 60-month or 5-year look-back period as well.

Another time a lady, Mrs. Jones, walked into my office. Her husband was in a nursing home, and she wanted to qualify him for Medicaid because she thought she had put her money away where it could not count as an asset. She wanted to know what kinds of questions they were going to ask. I explained everything to her and she felt she did not need anyone to help her, because she knew what she was, and was not, supposed to tell them. I told her to be honest, but do not divulge information—just answer the questions.

When she went to see the Medicaid qualifier and was asked if she had any personal property, she said yes. He was not going to ask her what those items were. They do not ask that question. They do not really want to know.

Mrs. Jones went on to say she was a little confused about her property, because she didn't know what to do with the two gold bullion bars that she had in her safe at home. The qualifier could not believe what he heard. Since she divulged this information, he wanted to know how much those gold bullion bars weighed. She told him the two bars weighed about twelve pounds. He quickly calculated 12 pounds times 16 ounces times $350 an ounce at that time. He told her that her husband would be disqualified for the next three to four years. He didn't need to ask any more questions after that. He wasn't going to ask her if she had a gold bullion bar at home as a personal property item. However, since she divulged that information, they could, and did, use it against her. The same goes for stamp collections, gun collections or knickknacks. The Medicaid qualifier isn't going to ask about those things. However, if you divulge it, Medicaid could require you to sell those items to pay your own nursing home expenses, and they are more than happy to have you do that.

Another thing that confuses a lot of people when they try to qualify for Medicaid is explaining that they gave money away to their children. As of this writing, you are allowed to give up to $12,000 a year away to each child, grandchild or their spouses. A mother and father could give a total of $24,000 to a child and his or her spouse. This can be done every year, and it is tax-free to the recipient. The important thing people tend to forget is that it is a tax law, not a Medicaid law.

If you have given money away to your children or you are planning to do so, it is because you do not need it and you want them to have it. It may not necessarily be the best option, because Medicaid can use that money against you as an asset if it was transferred within the past 60 months.

For example, a husband and wife have three children and they wanted to give money to each of them, so they gave $10,000 to each child 30 months ago. Then, 18 months ago they gave another $10,000 to each of their children. This year they gave another $10,000 to each, for a total of $90,000 in the past three years. If the husband has a stroke and goes into a nursing home, and the wife tries to qualify him for assistance because she does not have enough money to pay his expenses or wants to protect their remaining money, he may be disqualified (depending on when each gift of money was given).

Every time a gift of money is transferred to anyone other than a spouse, Medicaid starts the disqualification process from the date of that gift. For example, if I give my son a gift of $20,000 and then go into a nursing home three months later, Medicaid would then say that the $20,000 does count against me. If the state says the average monthly nursing home cost is $5,000 a month, then I would be ineligible for Medicaid for four months from the date of the gift. If the gift was $200,000, then I would be ineligible for Medicaid for 40 months from the date of the gift.

Remember that Medicaid law and tax laws are two different animals. It may not always be the best strategy to give your money away to your children early. In most cases this will hurt instead of help. The first thing that you lose when you give money away is **CONTROL**.

Chapter 7 The Deficit Reduction Act of 2005

"Good judgment comes from experience, and a lot of that comes from bad judgment."

- Will Rogers

In February 2006 President George W. Bush signed into law the Deficit Reduction Act of 2005, known now as the "DRA." This law cuts more than $40 billion over the next five years of federal funding for Medicare, Medicaid and several other programs. The act changes several different planning issues that were being used by many Americans in retirement. The biggest changes affect the look-back period, the use of annuities, the transfer penalty start date, community spouse income rules, home equity limits, and the treatment of investments in continuing care retirement communities (CCRCs).

What is the current look-back period?

The current look-back period becomes 60 months (5 years) instead of 36 months. This is the time Congress has set for all transfer of assets given away or transferred out of your name. Remember, you can hold your assets in whatever holdings you wish. You just can't give them away to someone else! Congress doesn't want someone to give away or transfer their entire assets one day and the next day qualify for Medicaid. The look-back period is being implemented differently in various states, so be aware. For example, New York's extension of the look-back period doesn't go into effect until February of 2009, while other states have already implemented and even back-dated it to encompass more applications that could possibly be denied. This extension of the look-back period will make the application process much more difficult and possibly result in many applications being denied for lack of documentation. This means you would have to produce the past five years of records instead of three. Just think how hard it may be for your children or loved one to organize these records, and think into the future about how your children keep their records today.

WHAT IS THE PENALTY PERIOD START DATE?

The penalty period is the period in which a Medicaid applicant is ineligible for Medicaid payment for long-term care services because the applicant has transferred assets for less than fair market value during the look-back period. What this means is that you cannot transfer an asset to another investment for less than it was worth just to qualify for Medicaid.

Before Congress passed the DRA, the penalty period began either when the transfer was made or on the first day of the next month. It was possible for the penalty period to expire before the person actually needed long term care help. **Under the DRA, the penalty period commences on the latter of the first day of the month in which the transfer was made or the date on which an individual is eligible for Medicaid benefits and would otherwise be receiving Medicaid but for the imposition of a penalty period.** This means the penalty period does not start until the nursing home resident is out of money and has no way to pay for however long the penalty period lasts.

This will likely have negative consequences for both nursing homes and their residents. Nursing homes will be on the hook (so to speak) for the care of the residents waiting out an extended penalty period. **Although nursing homes may not evict a resident who has nowhere else to go, they do not have to readmit a nonpaying resident who has been taken to a hospital and seeks readmission**. If nursing homes end up with many patients who need care and have no way to pay for it, they will seek other avenues. This may include "filial responsibility," meaning they can, and will, seek reimbursement from the patient's children. In the past, these laws were rarely enforced, but they do exist. They can hold adult children responsible for the financial support of indigent parents, and, in some cases, for their medical and nursing home costs.

Even worse, some states have passed laws that say if the transfer has taken place within five years they will assume it was done to establish Medicaid eligibility and can go after the value of the Medicaid care from the person who received the property or money.

Are There Changes to Personal Residence Rules?

Since passage of the DRA, non-countable, or "exempt" assets may now include the home site (personal residence) and contiguous real property up to $500,000 in equity.

DRA eliminates Medicaid eligibility for single individuals having more than $500,000 in equity value in a primary residence (individual states may choose to increase the exemption for the home to $750,000 in equity). An unlimited exemption for the home remains if it is occupied by a spouse, child under age 21, or a disabled/blind child of any age.

Permissible Uncompensated Transfers

The uncompensated transfers permitted under Medicaid remain unchanged by DRA. An uncompensated transfer of the home-site is an allowable transfer only when the home is transferred to one of the following:

1. Legal spouse
2. Natural, adopted, or stepchildren under 21 at time of transfer
3. Blind/disabled child of any age
4. Siblings who:
    a. Are co-owners of the home, and
    b. have been residing in the home for at least one year.

5. Natural, adopted or stepchild age 21 or over who:
   a. resided in the home for at least two years immediately before the applicant entered a nursing facility or request CAP, and
   b. provided care to the applicant to permit him or her to live at home, and
   c. provides documentation.

ARE THERE CHANGES TO RULES ON LIFE ESTATES?

The DRA essentially penalized creating any life estate other than through the purchase of a life estate in property which the Medicaid applicant/recipient then uses as his or her primary residence for at least one year.

The provision that will most commonly affect seniors is imposition of a transfer penalty for gifting a remainder interest (i.e., the interest in the property which begins upon the death of the life estate holder) in land to children. Individuals who wish to gift a remainder interest in property must do so well in advance of needing institutionalized care due to the new five-year look-back period. Otherwise, they will incur a significant penalty in Medicaid eligibility.

In reality, few seniors purchase life estates. Far more life estates are created by the gift of a remainder interest in property to children. Prior to the DRA, there were significant reasons to advise seniors to reserve a life estate:

1. Retained life estate interests offered important protections for the grantor against losing control of the residence.

2. Remainder interest holders benefit from a possible step-up in basis, reducing capital gains tax.

3. Transfer of a remainder interest resulted in a shorter Medicaid transfer penalty vs. transferring the entire property.

May potential Medicaid applicants still purchase life estate interests?

The DRA now penalizes purchasing a life estate unless it is in a residence and the applicant/recipient actually lives in the home for one year following the purchase. The DRA penalizes purchase of a life estate in any property other than a residence.

The DRA will significantly impact retained life estates. Although the retained life estate interest may still be Medicaid-exempt, the gift of the remainder will now result in a penalty beginning when the applicant is "otherwise eligible" for Medicaid.

ARE THERE STILL SPOUSAL IMPOVERISHMENT PROTECTIONS?

The DRA has little effect on the existing rules for married couples where one is applying for Medicaid and the community spouse seeks to protect some assets and income for his or her own support.

WHAT MEDICAID PLANNING TECHNIQUES ARE STILL AVAILABLE?

Many important elements of traditional "Medicaid planning" will remain unchanged. Married couples will still need to have a will with a discretionary trust for the benefit of the spouse if there is any likelihood of institutionalized care. "Will alternatives" can still be used to bypass the probate estate where there is any possibility of future estate recovery claims. The concept of transforming countable assets into exempt resources remains largely unchanged.

ARE SPECIAL NEEDS TRUSTS STILL ALLOWED?

The Deficit Reduction Act of 2005 does not directly affect existing rules and regulations that govern special needs trusts.

ARE THERE NEW RULES FOR PURCHASE OF AN ANNUITY?

One area in which the Deficit Reduction Act significantly changes planning for married couples is the purchase of an annuity. The Medicaid applicant or his or her spouse must disclose interest in an annuity.

The Act establishes new rules for the treatment of annuities, including that the state be named as the remainder beneficiary for certain annuities.

Under the Act, the purchase of an annuity is treated as an uncompensated transfer of assets unless: (1) the state is named as the first residuary beneficiary for an amount up to the total of all medical assistance provided to the annuitant, or (2) the state is named as the second residuary beneficiary, after the community spouse, a minor child or a disabled child.

Where the annuity is actuarially sound (i.e., it returns its entire value during the annuitant's life expectancy) it may not be considered an available resource for eligibility purposes. The client must purchase an immediate annuity rather than a deferred annuity in which payments under the contract must begin within one year following the initial premium payment.

One approach for short-term planning under the DRA involves the use of a short-term immediate annuity, whereby a person can become "otherwise eligible" by keeping less than the resource allowance and use the annuity as a source of funding for nursing home payments during the penalty period. For example, an individual who has assets worth $40,000 might transfer $20,000 to his children and at the same time purchase an immediate annuity that pays $5,000 per month for a period of four months. The individual then enters a nursing home. The penalty period begins upon the filing of an application for benefits. The nursing home payments are made through the four-month penalty by using the monthly annuity payments.

May we still get a reverse mortgage?

Reverse mortgages may become useful now that the Deficit Reduction Act reduces the options for intergenerational gifting. In light of the more severe restrictions on government long-term care assistance, children should closely account for the assistance they provide and treat such assistance as a loan, secured against assets (most likely the house) owned by the parent.

Did the Deficit Reduction Act eliminate use of trusts as a Medicaid planning tool?

Irrevocable grantor trusts, sometimes known as Medicaid asset protection trusts, remain viable as an advance-planning technique for individuals who can retain sufficient resources to pay for five years of care.

Factors to be considered include loss of control and income level of the senior. Include options that should be explored in spousal planning, caregiver agreements, use of DRA-compliant annuities or promissory notes, and the use of pooled trusts.

Chapter 8 Types of Annuities

"I'm not as concerned with the return **on** my money, as I am with the return **of** my money."
- Will Rogers

Types of Annuities

There are four types of annuities. It does not matter what brokers call them, what insurance companies call them, or what financial planners call them. There are only four defined types of annuities.

The first type is a variable annuity. Some people have shied away from this annuity in the past 10 years for a lot of different reasons. A variable annuity goes up and down with the market. It is very similar to a mutual fund. If you put $100,000 into a variable annuity and it goes up 10%, then you gain 10%. The following year, if the annuity goes down 15%, then you lose 15%. When you put money into a variable annuity, the funds are then broken up into different individual holdings. You may pick different funds that vary in risk. The problem is that in some cases your broker has made all these decisions based on what his or her company has suggested they go into. You and/or your broker can make changes to these options from year to year; however, making those changes in most cases is left up to the money manager on the account. This is why they are known for high fees.

Fees are involved in every variable annuity from every company. In addition, there are internal charges. Typical fees run from about 0.5% to as high as 4.5% to 5% per year. Those fees are either going to the company or to your broker. We all know that brokers do not call when your account goes down to say you lost money in the last quarter. If they do, you might move your money and they won't collect their commissions. Variable annuities can never be actuarially sound, because they have the potential to lose money. Variable annuities should be sold primarily to people in the work force who are in a position to take the risk of up and down market conditions and are willing to pay the fees.

The second type is a **fixed-rate annuity**, which works a lot like a CD. For example, if the annuity gives you a fixed rate of 5%, you get 5% interest for the life of the contract. There is no risk—the insurance company gives you that fixed rate year after year. The rate is not going to fluctuate up or down. Like all annuities, they are a contract sold by an insurance company.

The purchaser makes contributions (investments) into the annuity either as a lump sum (referred to as a single premium annuity) or over a period of time (known as a flexible premium annuity). The annuity returns the investment and any earnings to the owner at a later date. Like all annuities, contributions to a fixed annuity are made on an after-tax basis (unless the annuity is in a qualified plan or IRA), but the interest on the contributions accumulates tax-deferred until the time when the money is paid out. At payout time, the portion of the annuity payment attributable to the contribution is not taxable, but the rest of the distribution is taxable.

Fixed-rate annuities can be Medicaid friendly, if the company practices all the criteria required to make it Medicaid-compliant. If you are looking for Medicaid protection in an annuity, ask the company if the annuity is actuarially sound. Most companies that sell fixed-rate annuities are not Medicaid-compliant.

The third type is a **fixed-indexed annuity**, commonly known as an **equity-indexed annuity**. It is the most popular annuity today and has been since the year 2000. Indexed annuities have been around since the mid-1980s; however, they did not become popular until the fall of the stock market in 2000. Similar to fixed annuities, these products tie the rate of return to the performance of an equity index, such as Standard & Poor's 500 Composite Index.

Indexed annuities can be Medicaid-protected based on whether the company complies with all the required Medicaid protection criteria. An indexed annuity establishes a floor, or minimum amount of interest, that the company pays, which is around 3% today. Typically, it can be 1.5% to 3%. If the market goes down during the entire life of the contract, the insurance company will pay you that 3% minimum annualized return. ***You can never lose money***.

However, if the market goes up 7% in one year, the insurance company will give you that 7%. For example, if you put $100,000 into an annuity and the market goes up 7%, you would have a total of $107,000. You lock in that 7% gain. If the market goes down the following year, you would get no increase that year, but you would not lose any money like you would in the stock market. If the market goes up 6% the following year, 6% or $6,420 would be added to the $107,000 that was locked in the first year. This would bring your total to $113,420. The index annuity is an excellent tool for retirees, because it takes away any risk level. You share in the market gain, but you never share in the market loss. Your money is protected.

The worst-case scenario would be that you only earned the minimum interest. For example, you have a $100,000 annuity, and the market went down year after year for nine consecutive years, which, in this case, is the life of the contract. That has never happened, though theoretically it could. If the market went down nine consecutive years, you would be guaranteed a minimum 3% interest rate. At the end of the nine-year term, you would have a minimum of $127,000 in your account. It is a very good retirement vehicle.

The fourth type of annuity is the **single premium immediate annuity** (SPIA). When you put money into a SPIA, it will immediately annuitize or start a payout structure back to you based on your life expectancy. SPIA's are commonly used when someone is entering a nursing home, or when someone is looking for income. For example, you have a lump-sum payment from the sale of a home or you have a lump-sum of money and would like a monthly income from it. That money could be put into a SPIA,which would yield a guaranteed fixed interest rate and start a payout structure to pay you money and provide a monthly income stream. It could be a 5- or 10-year payout, or however long the money would last with the desired monthly payment.

When you look at an annuity as a retirement vehicle, there are certain things you should be aware of and ask your financial advisor about. One point is how soon after you die can your beneficiaries access the money. Certain annuities may have a 5- or 10-year payout, and your beneficiaries would be penalized if they withdrew that money sooner. It is important to ask about the terms of the payout, and if they would be entitled to the full amount of money. There may also be a penalty if you die within a certain period of time after buying that annuity. Look for annuities that do not have these penalties.

CAN I GET TO THE MONEY IF I NEED IT WHILE I'M STILL ALIVE?

Many annuity companies will put your money into an annuity and not allow you to take it out. You would be locking it up and throwing away the key for "X" amount of years. You want to avoid such annuities. You want to know that you can take your money out if necessary.

HOW DOES THE INSURANCE COMPANY MAKE MONEY?

There are only three ways that the insurance companies can limit your returns. Yes, you read this correctly. They are going to limit your returns. If there is no risk of any loss, then they have to insure themselves that they can always make more money than they are giving you. That means they will limit your return. The three ways are with: The **cap**, the **spread**, and the **participation rate**. Let's look at each one in more detail.

The **cap**: This is how much the insurance company is going to allow you to make. This cap can be figured by the month, the year, or even by the whole term of the contract. If you're capped by the month, for example, you may have a 3%-per-month crediting. This means in theory you could make 36% per year into your account. This is only a theory, because the market that it is credited to would have to grow 3% or higher each month, 12 months consecutively. This, to my knowledge, has never happened and I don't see it happening anytime soon. However, you could see returns well into double digits, as we did with this credit method over the past couple of years (2006, 2007).

The **spread**: This is simply a fee. Insurance companies don't call it a fee. However, I don't care how you slice it—it's a fee. The spread is the difference of what you are credited on your return minus the spread. For example: You may find a company that has a 1.25% spread. If the S&P 500 is the index that your policy credits to, and the growth was 8%, then you would credit 6.75%. This type of spread is based on the entire accumulated amount of your policy each year. For example: If your account balance at the end of the year is $200,000 and your spread is 1.25%, then you are charged $2,500. Spread may vary greatly from company to company and from policy to policy. Also you may find products and companies that have no spreads. One thing to always look for in a policy is, if your policy has a spread, can it change from year to year in your policy, and what are the maximum amounts it can go up to.

The **participation rate:** This is what percentage of the market returns the company is going to allow you to participate in. For example: If the S&P 500 goes up 10%, and you have an 80% participation rate, then your return would be 8%. Again, things to look for when you have a participation rate are: What is it the first year? Will or can it change? And how low can it go? What has the history of that particular company and policy been in the past (renewal rate)? In short, the ideal policy would be one with the following: No cap, no spread, and 100% participation rate, all locked in for the duration of the policy. I have never seen a policy with these qualities in all my years. You may find policies that may have only one of the methods, and then again you can find policies that have all three.

Let's look at a commonly sold policy in Example I:

Example I. 10% cap per year annual point to point
No spread for the first year, then
up to 3% thereafter.
100% participation rate first year,
then could change to as low as 50% thereafter.

- Let's assume the S&P 500 made 10% in year one and then again in year two. Your return would be 10% in year one (Great!)

Year two: 10% minus the spread of (let's say) 1%
=9% then a participation rate of 50%
=4.5% YOUR TOTAL RETURN

In another example, let's assume a policy with a cap of 12% annually, no spread (ever), and 100% participation rate for the life of the policy. Same situation: 10% gain in the S&P 500 for two years. Your return is 10% in year one and 10% in year two.

So the question that should be posed is why wouldn't everyone buy the second policy? Well, the answer is simple: The first policy pays a substantially larger commission to the agent, and the client was probably never informed of how it actually works. This is why the industry as a whole has become a playground for unscrupulous agents looking out only for themselves.

In my opinion, this type of annuity could and should be a part of every retiree's long-term planning for their money (especially for IRAs, 401(k)s and any type of qualified money). However, you now know the proper questions to ask before you purchase one:

1. What is the **cap** and how is it calculated?
2. What is the **spread** and how can it change?
3. What is the **participation rate** and how can it change?

What about the tax status?

Many people today, including retirees, are paying too much in taxes. Your money for retirement purposes is money that you are not using every year, year after year. It needs to have a tax-deferred and/or tax-free status. While you are not using that money, you are not paying income taxes on it. In 1936, Franklin Delano Roosevelt said, "The American public will never pay taxes on Social Security." However, in 1983, Congress changed the law to tax Social Security. In 1993, they changed it again so, on certain income thresholds, up to 85% of your Social Security can be taxable.

If you have money in CDs, money market accounts, or cash of any kind that is drawing interest every year, you pay tax on the interest growth. That would indicate you are using every portion of that interest every year. Most certainly you would not want to be paying taxes on money you are not using. However, 90% of Americans do. The government loves you for it. If you simply put your money in a tax-deferred status with annuities, you will earn more money faster through compounding of that interest. It may also reduce, if not eliminate, the taxes on Social Security.

Chapter 9 Annuities for Medicaid Planning Purposes

"Success is not measured by how much money you make or have, but rather by achieving the goals you've set for yourself." - **Joe Leonard**

Are annuities used for qualifying for Medicaid?

Yes, in many cases people can use annuities as an essential part of their retirement plans, including for long-term care planning and Medicaid. While the use of annuities is a valuable tool, you need to fully understand what you are getting and how annuities work for Medicaid planning purposes.

Where you live and whether you are married or single can play a big part in the specific use. While historically "immediate" annuities have been used as a Medicaid planning tool, other types of annuities can be converted to a payout later in the contract to accomplish the same effect. In the previous chapter we presented individual annuity types and their specific purposes. In its simplest terms, an immediate annuity is a contract you've made with an insurance company in which you give the company a certain amount of money, and the company in return agrees to pay you a monthly check for the remaining days of your life. This was, and still is, a way that people or individuals with assets in excess of the limits set by Medicaid may turn these assets into an income stream while avoiding a penalty for transferring the asset.

The Deficit Reduction Act has changed many of the requirements for annuities, making this a little harder to accomplish. Under this new law (which we covered in the previous chapter) an annuity must meet certain requirements in order to avoid a transfer penalty:

- The annuity must be actuarially sound. This means that the annuity must be paid out under the purchaser's life expectancy and the payments must be equal to or greater than the cost of the annuity. You cannot transfer money to an annuity for Medicaid qualification purposes and suffer a loss by doing it. That would disqualify it.
- The payment must begin immediately when it is converted to this type of annuity. You cannot have a deferred payment at a later date and/or you cannot have a balloon payment option. (Ballon payment options were allowed in many states prior to 2005.)
- The annuity must be irrevocable once it is annuitized under this option, meaning that not even you can change or cancel it.
- Unless there is a spouse or a minor or disabled child, the state must be named as the remainder beneficiary (the person or entity that gets the leftover money) up to the amount of Medicaid that was provided. This is being challenged in many states today and from my understanding it only applies if you have started the annuity after going into long-term care and applying for Medicaid assistance.

The best use of an annuity for Medicaid planning is perhaps made by married couples, especially for the at-home spouse and his or her financial well-being. The immediate annuity allows for the couple to turn their excess assets into an income for the at-home spouse, allowing the other to qualify for Medicaid. If the at-home spouse purchases an annuity that meets all the requirements from the Deficit Reduction Act, then he or she will receive the income and not have to contribute to the cost of long-term care. However, under the new laws and amendment to the the Act in 2006, the spouse will have to name the state as the remainder beneficiary. This would only occur if she or he died before the guaranteed payments under the annuity had expired.

Under the Act, annuities for single individuals have been less useful. Once an individual enters long-term care and buys an annuity for Medicaid-qualifying purposes, he or she must receive the payment equally, and the payment will count as income and be used to pay the nursing home first. Once the purchaser dies, the remaining amount would go to the state first to pay any unpaid nursing home cost and then to the beneficiaries.

While immediate annuities can still be a very powerful tool in the right circumstances, they must be distinguished from variable and deferred annuities, which are not used for Medicaid planning purposes. Also be aware that the use of annuities for Medicaid planning varies from state to state, so be sure you consult with a qualified professional.

Annuities for Medicaid Planning Purposes

What are Medicaid annuities, and do they really exist? Of the many types of annuities, there really is no such thing as a Medicaid annuity. Medicaid does not issue annuities. The layman terminology is a Medicaid-planning, Medicaid-friendly, or Medicaid-compliant annuity, but the legal term is an annuity that is actuarially sound. What makes an annuity actuarially sound will be defined later in this chapter.

The use of annuities for Medicaid planning has been prevalent for years now. However, each state varies slightly on how it accepts, qualifies, or disqualifies an annuity for Medicaid purposes. In general, annuities for Medicaid planning exist in all 50 states.

Who Sells Actuarially Sound Annuities?

An actuarially sound annuity can be sold by any licensed life insurance agent. These are very specific annuities, and your general health insurance agent, life insurance agent, or broker may not be well versed in how these annuities work. The best advice is to seek a professional who works strictly in annuities that are actuarially sound. You can contact someone who is knowledgeable in that area, such as an elder law attorney, an elder care planner, or a certified senior advisor. Typically, brokers do not sell actuarially sound annuities. There are many complexities regarding issues, such as which annuities do what they are supposed to and which ones do not. There are thousands of different national annuity companies, but there may be only a select few that are actuarially sound for Medicaid planning.

What makes an annuity actuarially sound? What are the differences, and what makes an annuity Medicaid-protected or Medicaid-compliant? The first and foremost issue is that the annuity company must use the life expectancy chart established by the Social Security Administration. This means someone, an actuary, at the Social Security office is responsible to calculate when you are going to die. Every insurance company also has its own actuary. For example, under Medicaid guidelines, a 70-year-old female's life expectancy is 16 years. However, if the insurance company from which you purchased an annuity has its own actuary table, it may say the same female has a 20-year life expectancy. It clearly does not use the same life expectancy table. Therefore, it is not a Medicaid or actuarially sound annuity. Many people ask why an insurance company would want to say you are going to live 20 years when the Medicaid or Social Security guidelines state you are only going to live 16 years. The insurance company would be more than happy to hold your money in an annuity and earn interest on it for 20 years vs. the 16 years of a Medicaid-compliant annuity. The first issue that disqualifies an annuity for Medicaid is not being actuarially sound.

A Medicaid-friendly annuity will also allow for a change of annuitant from one spouse to the other before it is annuitized to protect the spouse at home. A question for a married couple to consider is, which one would go into long-term care first. Since no one knows the answer, you need to be able to change ownership from one person to the other to protect the remaining money for the spouse who is at home, so that spouse does not become impoverished.

A Medicaid-compliant annuity must be irrevocable and unassignable once it is annuitized. This means if someone is in a nursing home or in a long-term care situation, once the annuity has been annuitized for the spouse at home, it is drawing an income. This makes the principal of the annuity exempt from Medicaid's using it as an asset, because it cannot be altered in any way. Once you convert it into an income for yourself, if someone is in a nursing home or long-term care situation, it cannot fluctuate. The amount of the annuitized income cannot be changed.

Annuities are usually purchased to provide a source of income for retirement and are casually used to shelter assets so that individuals purchasing them are eligible for Medicaid. In order to avoid penalizing annuities already purchased as part of the retirement plan, but to capture those annuities that abuse the shelter of assets, a determination must be made with regard to the ultimate purpose of the annuity. You cannot purchase an annuity for a lesser amount than the fair market value just to protect it from Medicaid. For example, if you had $100,000 in a money market account, you could not purchase a $100,000 annuity for $90,000. You can purchase an annuity for the same amount of money, which means you cannot lose money in the transaction. You cannot shelter money and take a loss to simply protect it for Medicaid purposes.

If the expected return on the annuity is commensurate with a reasonable estimate of the life expectancy of the beneficiary, the annuity can be actuarially sound. For the purpose of determining Medicaid eligibility, an actuarially sound annuity is an insurance product designed to pay off the entire asset value over the actual, or expected, lifetime of the annuitant. The guaranteed period of payments must end during the annuitant's expected lifetime. The total of the proceeds must be designed to be dispersed in a substantial, equal, periodic payment with no anticipated lump-sum payment. The only allowable lump-sum payment is the committed value of the guaranteed payments remaining when the annuitant dies prior to the end of the guaranteed period.

For example, if a 70-year-old single man purchases a $100,000 annuity and his life expectancy is 16 years from the date the annuity was issued, the annuity will allow the schedule of payments to be calculated from age 70, even though he went into the nursing home at age 85. An actuarially sound Medicaid annuity uses the life expectancy from the date the contract was issued. If his life expectancy was 16 years when the annuity was purchased at age 70, when he goes into a nursing home at age 85, he has to start drawing money from that annuity to annuitize it. Since he does not have a spouse to whom he could transfer the annuity, he has to draw that $100,000 out over a 16-year period. Using simple math, he would have to draw out equal payments of $6,250 per year from that annuity for 16 years, which would be considered income and go directly to the nursing home. If he dies in the nursing home anytime within that 16-year period, the remaining amount of funds left in the annuity would go to the beneficiaries, not to the nursing home. In the case of a married couple in that same situation, the $100,000 could be transferred to the at-home spouse to protect the asset for that spouse.

Single Premium Immediate Annuity (SPIA)

The single premium immediate annuity (SPIA) is another type of annuity commonly used for Medicaid protection. When you put money into this annuity, it immediately starts paying out to you based on your life expectancy. Can you purchase a SPIA that is Medicaid-friendly when you go into a nursing home? The answer is yes. You could enter a nursing home, take your remaining amount of money out before you qualify for Medicaid, put it into a SPIA, and you may possibly be able to qualify for Medicaid. The reason I say "possibly" is that individual Medicaid qualifiers evaluate situations differently. If you wait until something happens to put money into a Medicaid protected annuity, it will be up to the individual qualifier to determine whether you did that simply to circumvent the system or as a pre-planning measure. Pre-planning always works; post-planning rarely works. Planning ahead always makes life simpler than post-planning. Most post-planning will cost you something when you put money into a SPIA. Whether an attorney, a broker, or a financial planner does it, typically, a fee is involved to initiate trying to save some of your remaining asset.

My financial advisor told me that if I go into a nursing home, all I have to do is annuitize or start drawing payments from my annuity, and it will be Medicaid-protected. Is that correct?

No, an annuity has to follow all of the guidelines that were presented previously. Simply putting money into a payment structure does not make it Medicaid-qualified. It has to be calculated for the life expectancy of the individual at that time. It does not have to be irrevocable, but it has to be unassignable, non-transferable, and with no balloon payment option. If it follows all those criteria, it may be determined to be actuarially sound. However, if you are doing this at the time of going into a nursing home, most states and most qualifiers will still disqualify that annuity for Medicaid purposes. You may try to argue your case at the state or federal level, but, again, it will cost money. Pre-planning always works, and post-planning rarely, if ever, works. This is why one of the new laws passed in the Deficit Reduction Act stipulates that if you start an annuity for Medicaid planning purposes (after you're in a long-term care situation) you must name the state the beneficiary.

Is it true that if I buy an annuity, the insurance company keeps all my money when I die?

Most of the annuities sold today do not keep your money. There are annuities called life-paid annuities, which were very commonly sold 10 to 15 years ago. If you gave your money to an insurance company for a life-paid annuity, it agreed to pay you back "X" amount of dollars monthly. For example, if you gave $100,000, it might have paid you $600 per month for life. If you were 65 years old when you put this money in, it would give you

$600 every month for the rest of your life. If you died five years later, you would not have received back all of the $100,000 that you put in. At that time, the insurance company would have kept the remaining amount of money. It was betting on you dying early, while you were betting on living longer. If, however, you had lived to be 95 years old, you would have collected a lot more than $100,000, and the insurance company would have lost money.

You can be sure that insurance companies statistically never lose. Putting money into a life-paid annuity is the wrong thing to do, simply because you are betting on an unknown factor. You are betting that you are going to live longer and receive more money from the insurance company. Keep in mind, the insurance company bases everything on statistics and averages. They calculate that you are only going to live "X" amount of years, and you are hoping to live longer. If your family history indicates that everyone in your family lives to be 100 and you want to put money in a life-paid annuity at age 60, you may have a better chance of collecting more from the insurance company than you initially put in. However, statistically, the insurance company always wins. It is much better to put money into annuities that will pay back your principal and interest on a regular basis. When you pass away, the remaining amount of money goes to your beneficiaries.

Those are the types of annuities most commonly sold today. Some annuities are still considered life-paid annuities, but for retirees, they would not be in their best interest.

AM I TOO OLD TO GET ANNUITIES ?

Absolutely not. A common misconception I have heard from clients is that they are in their 70s, 80s, or 90s and think they are too old to buy annuities. That is not correct. People in their 100s can purchase annuities if they wish. Insurance companies may have stipulations that some products are only available up to certain age limits. However, you can purchase single premium immediate annuities up to age 110 if you so choose. You are never too old to invest your money for safety and protection.

I'M GOING TO SPEND ALL OF MY MONEY BEFORE I DIE.

I hear this from clients all the time. They say they are already 80 years old, and they want to spend all of their money before they die. My question to them is: "What day is that?" If they can tell me the day they are going to pass away, I can make sure their money runs out the day before. That is everyone's ultimate plan. They want to run out of money one day and pass away the next day. They would never have any worries about outliving their money. They would never have any worries about to whom they are going to leave their excess money. Unfortunately, no one knows when he or she is going to die. The best plan is to make sure you have your money available when you need it. If money is left over, make sure it is properly designated for your beneficiaries.

Chapter 10 IRAs

Question: How long does it take for your heirs to spend their inheritance? The average time, if you leave $1 million or less, is nine months.

- Source: AARP, 2004

IRAs are individual retirement accounts. Many people have various individual retirement accounts, such as a 401(k), 403(b), or 457, which they convert into another financial vehicle at the time of retirement. This money is considered qualified money, or any money on which taxes have not yet been paid. Non-qualified money is any money on which the taxes have been paid.

Since the taxes have not been paid on any of the qualified money put into an IRA, there are two stipulations for withdrawal. One, you cannot withdraw the money until you are age 59 1/2. Two, at age 70 1/2 you will be required to draw out a certain percentage of money. That percentage is called the required minimum distribution, or RMD. It is calculated according to government tables. Typically, if you divide the amount of money in your IRA by 27.2, that will be the amount of your first required minimum distribution. Every year your required minimum distribution increases percentage-wise. You must take it, so eventually it will start diminishing the longer you live. Based on your required minimum distributions, if you live to be age 85, 90, or 95, you may have drawn out all of your money.

As you withdraw your required minimum distribution each year, you have to pay the tax on that money. It is counted as ordinary income so, whatever income bracket you are in at that time, you will pay the tax to the government. Basically, the government is saying that by the age of 70 1/2, you are now old enough to start paying taxes on the money they allowed you to put away tax-free for that period of time.

The biggest question from most clients, once they reach age 70 1/2 and are required to take their distribution, is where can they put that money so they do not have to take it out. The answer is *nowhere.* IRAs must be drawn out at age 70 1/2, or you will pay a very hefty penalty. In some cases the penalty can be as high as 50%, so you will want to take it out.

Once that money is drawn out and the taxes have been paid, it becomes non-qualified money. You may now put that money wherever you wish. You can spend it, gift it away, or reinvest it in non-qualified accounts. Most people tend to take their RMDs toward the end of the year. They use the money to buy Christmas gifts, go on a vacation, or do whatever they want. It is fun money for them.

The inherent problem with most IRAs is what would happen if you do not use the money, you do not pass it down to a spouse, or your spouse does not use all the money. Prior to January 2003, if that money was left to your children, they could only take it out in two different distributions. One was a lump-sum, and about 95% of the time children would take it out in a lump-sum if you allowed them to. Alternatively, they could take it out in a five-year payout. Most of them took it in a lump-sum, because they wanted to spend it.

A good question to consider is how long will it take your children to spend your money. On average, we have found if the amount is less than $1 million, most of the time that money will be spent in nine months or less. That is very disturbing. The generation of 65 years and older is a generation of savers. The next generation of 40- to 65-year olds is a generation of spenders. The generation of 18- to 40-year olds is a generation of borrowers. They do not even spend their own money.

In August 2003, Congress changed the IRA laws and allowed different types of distributions. Fewer than 10% of the people who come into our office know that the IRA distribution laws have changed, and they now have different distribution methods they can select. Congress passed legislation that states you no longer have to pass your IRA down to your children upon your and your spouse's death. You can now pass your IRA down through a stretch distribution. Also, you can pass your IRA down not only to your children, but to your grandchildren. Before 2003, you could not do that.

This new distribution method is known by three names: a stretch IRA, a multi-generational IRA, or a family legacy IRA. They are all the same. You may now select the distribution method as to how your funds will be passed down after death, rather than your children choosing it. For example, if you had two children and two grandchildren, upon the death of the second spouse, you could select that any remaining money in your IRAs would be handed down in equal shares—25% to one child, 25% to the other child, and 25 % to each grandchild. You can allow them to take it out in a lump-sum, in a five- or 10-year payout, a lifetime payout, or any payout structure you wish. If you select a lifetime payout for all four, the oldest child is going to get a higher distribution, because he or she has fewer years to get that distribution, and so on. The grandchildren, however, have a lot more years of distribution, which means that money will continue earning interest tax-deferred, and they will have many more years of compounding and interest growth.

Maximize the Power of a Stretch IRA

As you can see, starting with $100,000 the stretch IRA will end up to be over $1.8 million in total distribution. Many people have asked why Congress would pass such laws. Previously, if you were over the age of 70 1/2, you could not make any changes to your IRAs. If you look at some common factors about our representatives, you will notice that many are over 70 1/2 years of age. There was one thing that they could do—they could change the law, and they did.

One good feature of a stretch IRA distribution is that you, not your children, select how your IRA will be distributed after your death. Upon the death of both spouses, there is no way the children can change the distribution method that you have set up. I tell the children that if they do not like the distribution method, they need to take that up with mom or dad. If they have ulterior motives and want the money in a different distribution other than what you selected, then you probably designated it the correct way.

Chapter 11 A World of Terror-Terrorist Attacks Will it Happen Again? What Will Happen to the Markets?

Our world has been forever changed by the events of September 11, 2001, and of the events of the recent past. The long-lasting effects are still yet to be determined. The short-term effects were devastating to some of our nation's retirees. In several cases, the immediate downtrend of the market caused losses in portfolios upwards of 50% to 70%. The average investor could not continue to just hold out and wait for the upside to return. Many of you may have heard these clichés: "Don't worry, just hang in there," "We're in it for the long haul," "It's only a paper loss." What this meant in hindsight is that no one really knew what was going to happen and how severe it could be. My question, however, is, how did this affect long- and short-term goals for you and your money? When your broker or financial planner was telling you to just hang in there, did he or she tell you how long to wait? What is the acceptable time? I have had several hundred experiences since 9-11 with clients where the only reason they were being told to "hang in there" was for their financial planner's/broker's interest, not their own. The broker simply didn't want to lose the account or the commission. This sickens me about our industry today and makes it harder and harder for the professionals who do have the client's best interest at heart.

I've been asking this question to groups of seniors for the

past few years at almost all of my speaking events: "How many of you believe in your lifetime we will see another attack on our country like 9-11?" Now remember these people are from age 55 to 85. With thousands of people asked this question, approximately 90% feel it's coming. What effect will that have on our market, our economy, and our children and grandchildren? How does it affect you and how does this influence where you keep your money today?

This reminds me of my grandfather and for that matter, my father, who either grew up in the Depression or as a Depression baby. They didn't trust the banks or our government system. They kept money where it was always accessible. This might be in a coffee can in the cupboard, buried in the back yard or under the mattress. Does the threat of a terrorist attack on our country or its citizens influence where and what products you keep your money in? How fast could you access your money? How safe is it? And would the quick downfall of the market affect your ability to access it? I don't know if anyone can even give you a proper answer to these questions.

Today we live in a world of uncertainty. My personal belief is that people should lean more toward the safety and protection of their assets than the growth of those assets.

Chapter 12 Life Insurance

"The aging of America's Baby Boomers is the most pressing national issue of the century" **- Source: *Harvard Generations* policy journal, Winter 2004**

If someone came into my office and told me that seniors or retirees need to be concerned about buying more life insurance, I would escort the person out faster than he or she walked in. As a whole, buying life insurance as a senior or a retiree is probably one of the worst investments most people could make, whether whole life, universal, or term life. However, there are particular needs people may want to consider with certain life insurance. One of the reasons people buy life insurance is to pay off debt they have accrued. A younger couple with children may need college tuition, they may have car payments, and even a lifestyle to uphold. Life insurance is a very good product to have, and most of the time the proper life insurance is term life insurance.

There are three types of life insurance: Term life, universal life and whole life. Many years ago whole life policies were sold the most. They built a little equity, and you could pay up that policy. However, it took a very long time. It only accumulated a couple of percent in interest, and only made interest on a portion of the principal that you put in.

Universal life combines the cash value of whole life with term life. Premiums are deposited in the cash account after the insurance company deducts its fee and monthly cost for the term coverage.

Term life is the best buy most of the time. It is a policy that terminates at the end of a specified number of years, with no equity in that policy whatsoever. For example, if a 35-year-old male in good health bought a $100,000 20-year term life policy, that policy would end in 20 years on his 55th birthday. There is no cash value accumulated. He had the coverage of a $100,000 death benefit. In the event he died before age 55, his beneficiary would have received $100,000. Life insurance is a tax-free distribution, so that $100,000 would be a net amount to his spouse, children, or whomever he designated as his beneficiaries. He was buying that term insurance during the period of time he thought he needed to pay off debt, so it protected his family from a loss of income.

At age 55 when his children are probably grown and gone, he most likely does not have the educational debt to pay off. He may have also paid off his home by that point, so he would not have a mortgage. The $100,000 may have been just enough for his wife to get by on, if there was a lack of his income or pension. Most people try to buy enough term insurance to carry them to whatever age they plan to retire. Their term policy will typically run out in that length of time.

There is a very easy method to figure out how much term life insurance a working person or a retiree should carry. It is called the DIME method. DIME is an acronym for debt, income, mortgage and education. To calculate the amount of insurance you need, write each letter vertically down a sheet of paper (see Fig. 1). You will enter a total amount next to each letter, so you have four rows of numbers. First, add up the total of all debt from car loans, credit cards, etc. Write that total next to the "D," for example, $20,000. Second, take your annual income and multiply it times five years. Write that total next to the "I," for example, $300,000. Third, write down the amount that is still owed on your mortgage next to the "M," for example, $100,000. Fourth, if you have children who still need to be educated, multiply the number of children by $60,000, and write that total next to the "E." For example, if you have three children, the total is $180,000. Add up the four rows of numbers, and the total will give you the exact amount of term life insurance you should have during your working years before retirement. In this example it would be $600,000.

Figure 1

D	$ 20,000
I	$300,000
M	$100,000
E	$180,000
	$600,000

You may also want to consider term life insurance at retirement. You may not have the mortgage or education expenses, and you may have some income loss with a pension. Your pension may not be transferable to your spouse, or your pension may cease at death. Typically, the best time to buy term life insurance is between the ages of 50 and 65. It is also a good idea to buy a term policy that will last until you are 80 or 85 years old. Those term policies are going to be a little more expensive, because the older you are when you buy life insurance, the more it is going to cost on a per-thousand basis.

Another type of life insurance you may want to consider is single paid-up premium life. It is designed for seniors or retirees to purchase when they simply want to leave their money as an inheritance. If your children were asked if they would like their inheritance to be taxable or non-taxable, they would, of course, say non-taxable. Single paid-up premium life is a tax-free benefit to your heirs upon your death. Death benefits are not federally taxed. For example, if a 70-year-old single female retiree wanted to buy a $100,000 single paid up premium life policy, her death benefit from day one would be $100,000. If three months go by and she passes away, her beneficiaries get the total $100,000 tax-free.

The best thing about these paid-up premium life policies is that you have access to your money at any time without penalty. This means when you put that $100,000 into the policy, it is also going to be accruing interest, typically between a 3% and 7%

interest rate per year. As that principal grows with interest, your death benefit also increases. If 10 years go by and you want to take out $40,000 to buy a brand new Cadillac because you do not care if this money gets passed down to your children, you can take that $40,000 out in a lump-sum. It is considered an accelerated death benefit. It is a tax-free distribution to you that will reduce your death benefit by the amount you withdrew.

Another possible scenario may be that you do not need to pull the money out in a lump-sum but, in five or 10 years down the road, withdraw $1,000 a month as income. It may be annuitized or put into a payment schedule just like an annuity or any other financial product. It is paying you $1,000 a month and reducing your death benefit in conjunction with the amount withdrawn. However, that $100,000 benefit you are receiving is a tax-free distribution because, again, it is an accelerated death benefit. It gives you the freedom to use that money when you want with no penalties. You are not tying it up for a certain period of time but, if you do want to use it, you can.

If you do not use the money, it will pass directly to your heirs as a tax-free benefit, and it includes the interest growth of that money. For example, if 20 years elapsed and you never withdrew any money, that $100,000 death benefit may have grown to $250,000. That $250,000 goes to your heirs tax-free. The downside of having a life insurance product like this for most seniors or retirees is that it is a life insurance product, which means you have to qualify for it with a medical exam. The three major conditions that disqualify people from buying a paid-up life policy is if you have had a heart attack, have ongoing cancer treatments, or are an insulin-dependent diabetic. If you do not have any of those three, there is a very good chance you will qualify for this type of life insurance program. It is one of the most lenient underwriting life insurance programs in existence. It may be something people would like to consider for money they are planning to leave to their heirs.

Chapter 13 Estate Taxes, Gift Taxes, and Taxes on Social Security

"By 2030 the demographics of 32 states will resemble those of Florida today."
- Source: U.S. Census Bureau

Despite its premise to simplify the tax code, Congress' never-ending changes to our nation's estate and gift tax code have made it too complicated for most people to understand. Every year, they discuss estate taxes and gift taxes, and make them more and more complicated, so the average person has no idea what to do.

What are federal estate taxes?

The federal estate tax and gift tax are known as transfer taxes. They are taxes on your right to give away money and/or property to others. The gift tax is a tax you have to pay while you are still living. The estate tax is a tax on your right to leave property to others upon your death. There are two philosophies for some people. One is to give your money away while you are alive, which could encompass gift taxes. The other is that you do not care what happens to your money after you are gone, so, on your passing, your estate may be subject to a federal estate tax. For example, my dad's philosophy was that when he was gone, the kids could deal with it, which could have encompassed federal estate taxes.

Why should I be concerned about these types of taxes?

In effect, the federal estate and gift taxes constitute a double tax on your assets. Not only are your assets taxed when you first earn them by the application of income tax, but they are also taxed when you pass away. Your lifetime savings can be taxed a second time when you pass them on to your children. Without proper planning, these taxes can take up to 50% or more of your life savings and that should be a major concern to everyone involved.

Is there a way to avoid these taxes?

Fortunately, the federal estate and gift taxes are mostly avoidable for those who take the time and effort to plan their estates. Unfortunately, most people do not take the time. Therefore, if they have a taxable estate, they risk the danger of having to pay otherwise unnecessary taxes.

How do I know if I have a taxable estate?

For the most part, this is an individual issue. Whether or not you have a taxable estate depends initially on how much property you own at the time of your death. The size of your taxable estate is calculated by first adding up the current, fair market value of everything you own. These are your assets, which include such things as your home, other real estate, checking and savings accounts, business holdings, CDs, stocks, mutual funds, bonds, IRAs including 401(k), 403(b), pension programs, and personal property. Your mortgage and death expenses are then subtracted from your total assets. Most people do not realize that, in addition to all of your real assets, you have death benefits from insurance policies which will be included in calculating the size of your taxable estate. Any taxable gifts made during your entire life will also be added, because federal tax laws are written to make sure you do not avoid estate taxes at your death by giving everything away while you are still alive.

What is the applicable exclusion amount?

Rather than taxing all estates no matter how small, Congress has determined that at death everyone is entitled to transfer a given amount of property estate tax-free. This is called the estate tax exclusion, and more commonly called the applicable exclusion amount. The actual amount of the exclusion has been changed frequently by Congress. It is also reduced by the value of any taxable gifts made during the taxpayer's lifetime. In 2006, you had a $2 million exemption. In the year 2007, the exemption went up to $2.5 million, in 2008 it is $3 million, and in the year 2009 it will be a $3.5 million exemption. Then in 2010, it goes away for one year, and there is no tax for that one year. In 2011, it is scheduled to be reinstated at a lower amount of a $1 million exemption.

How are gift taxes calculated?

Congress has decided that lifetime gifts which exceed the annual gift tax exemption of $12,000 in a calendar year, as of this writing, will be subject to gift taxes. Gifts that are below the annual exemption are tax-free. The gift is tax-free to the individual receiving it and tax-free to the person giving it. The annual exemption is indexed for inflation. It began in 1997, so it is necessary to check with your estate planning attorney or your financial advisor for the current annual exemption amount, because each year it goes up. Even if a taxable gift is made, the tax is not immediately due. Instead, each time a taxable gift is made, the taxpayer is required to file a gift tax report with the IRS which keeps track of them. At the taxpayer's death, all taxable gifts made during the taxpayer's lifetime are added together to determine the total amount of taxable gifts. The amount of all lifetime taxable gifts are then subtracted from the applicable exclusion to determine how much property your estate is entitled to pass on at your death estate tax-free.

What happens if I have a taxable estate?

If you have a taxable estate, federal estate taxes are due and must be paid no later than nine months after the date of death to avoid penalties and interest. Additionally, the tax must be paid in cash. If your estate is going to be subject to estate tax, you need to plan to provide this needed cash through assets that are readily and easily converted to cash. For example, if you had property valued at $2.5 million in 2006, you would have $500,000 of a taxable estate at your death, because the exemption is $2 million. The tax would be 50% of the $500,000 which is $250,000 due within nine months after death. In this scenario, you would have to liquidate some of that property to pay the tax. You only have nine months to pay the estate tax before you have to start paying interest and penalties.

The need to raise cash quickly is frequently the reason that estates are forced to rapidly sell assets, which may include businesses and all other property. They may possibly have to be sold at below-market prices, because of the need to liquidate and get cash quickly to pay the government. Even if your estate is liable for estate taxes, there is still some good news. Usually these taxes can be paid in installments for a period of many years. In some circumstances, the government allows very favorable interest rates during the payment period, if taxes are due. An estate planning attorney will be able to help you select the best way to pay any taxes.

WHAT IF THE FEDERAL ESTATE TAX IS REPEALED?

Many people have heard that the federal estate tax exclusion amount is poised to rise drastically in the next few years, which would render many estates free from federal estate taxation. You may also have heard that Congress may eliminate the federal estate tax entirely. Regardless of such speculation, sound estate planning still requires implementation of strategies to avoid federal estate taxes for a variety of reasons. First, regardless of what happens in the future, the federal estate tax is still in existence today. Good planning is always based on the situation that exists today with an eye on tomorrow.

The reality is that, if your estate is taxable today, and you or your spouse dies today, you will have lost significant tax avoidance opportunities to which your families are entitled. Second, Congress is constantly tinkering with the exemption amount, and how the law applies today will, in all likelihood, change tomorrow. A good estate plan will be solid enough to avoid the taxes that would be imposed if you would die today, while still remaining flexible enough to be amended to keep up with the changes in the law. Estate planning should not be viewed as a one-time affair. Instead, a good estate plan should be periodically reviewed to keep it current with changes in the family as well as changes in the law. The speculation that the estate tax will be eliminated is not a valid reason to forego implementing an estate plan.

Speculation concerning the future should never be a substitute for planning what is needed today. Furthermore, even if the federal estate tax is fully revoked, history has taught us that Congress would probably reenact it in a few years. It is the adage, "Giveth with one hand and taketh away with the other." We know that if they eliminate one taxation law, they will probably implement another taxation law in a different area to compensate.

Chapter 14 Risk- What Is It? Do I Have Too Much?

"It is possible to fail in many ways...while to succeed is possible only in one way."
- Aristotle (384 BC- 322 BC)

As the old saying goes: "No risk, no reward. No pain, no gain." The list of clichés can go on and on.

What is risk?

The dictionary defines "risk" as: The chance of something going wrong; the danger that injury, damage, or loss will occur." In finance, it means the possibility of loss in an investment or speculation. To me it simply means: How much of the investment will you stand to lose? The problem with the risk and reward relationship is that the reward is always a "potential" reward. In a perfect world, there would be no risk. Still, if you're an investor in the market, you need a way to figure out what that reward should be. Fortunately, there is a quick way you can get a reading on an investment's potential reward to see if it is in line with the risk.

First, you need to determine a benchmark. Many investors use the U.S. Treasury Bonds for this, since they are backed by the "full faith and credit" of the U.S. government. If you determine that you can get a risk-free return on a Treasury bond, of let's say 5%, then this becomes your baseline. Any risk that you may now incur must return more than 5%. Anything over a 5% return is now known as the "risk premium." The question you need to ask yourself when looking at a particular investment is this: Is the "risk premium" high enough so that it is worth risking the loss of my money?

Do I have too much risk?

In my opinion, most people have too much risk. However, I also believe that it is inherent in us as Americans to gamble or take risks for the big return. You should always only risk what you are completely willing to lose, especially since you and I have no control over what the market does. For example, in the few days of writing this section of the book, the market has lost 380 points in one day, gained 200 back the next, and then was virtually flat the next. No one can even begin to say why. To me, it's like a roller coaster that goes very slowly as it rises, then picks up speed as it rushes down, then up, then down, but eventually the ride comes to an end. Your heart is beating fast, you had an adrenaline rush, but at some phase you're glad to be done. When young we loved the roller coaster ride; however the older we get the more we enjoy the "tea-cup" ride or just a calm walk. Only **you** can determine when it is time to get off the roller coaster. Not me!

I see many clients who have risks only for the sole purpose of their broker's well-being. I know many brokers will read this and think it's crap, but in my opinion it's 100% true. Here is an example of 10 years of two different accounts:

	Account #1	Account #2
Yr. 1	7%	+9%
Yr. 2	7%	-12%
Yr. 3	7%	-23%
Yr. 4	7%	-18%
Yr. 5	7%	+50%
Yr. 6	7%	+7%
Yr. 7	7%	+5%
Yr. 8	7%	+11%
Yr. 9	7%	+21%
Yr. 10	7%	+22%
Total Growth	70%	72%

Which one do you choose? When asked 95% of people say they want account #2.

Now let's put the actual dollar amount of $100,000 in each account and see what happened:

Account #1
now has $200,000 @ 7% over 10 years with compounding.

Account #2
now has $167,242.

Both accounts have a 70%-plus growth However, the volatile account went down early in the 10 years and had to climb back before it was in positive territory again. If you include the fees associated with account #2, it now has only $142,000. Yet you're still told by your broker that your account is up 70%.

Here is Account #2.

$100,000	+ 9%
$109,000	-12%
$95,920	-23%
$73,859	-18%
$60,565	+50%
$90,847	+ 7%
$97,206	+ 5%
$102,066	+11%
$113,293	+21%
$137,084	+22%
$167,242	

It's the tortoise and the hare. *Now* which account do you want? That's a $32,758 difference of better growth in account #1 vs. #2. The biggest difference in my opinion is this: One had risk and one did not.

These figures are account returns that transpired in actual client returns.

DO I REALLY NEED RISK AT THIS POINT IN LIFE?

There are a lot of factors to consider to accurately answer this question. What stage of your life are you in? How much money do you have? Have much of it do you need? And most importantly, how much are you willing to lose? I find in general with clients I have worked with over the past 14 years, that the older they get the less willing they are to take risks and also the less willing they are to part with whatever they have accumulated.

My formula for the average retiree is simple. Beyond the income needs of your funds, the excess funds that are totally discretionary should be risked at these percentages: if you're 65 years young, then 65% of your total non-essential cash funds should be completely invested at a NO-RISK level. These types of investments would be products such as annuities (fixed, or indexed only), money markets, Treasury bonds, or simply cash. Approximately 35% of your non-essential living money could be and should be in risk accounts for better potential growth. If you're 75 then the split should be 75% risk free to 25% at risk.

Following this formula will also lower your outflow of cash. This means that you will not be paying anywhere near the amount of dollars in fee-based accounts. On average, this will save you approximately **1.5%** to **3%** per year in outgoing fees. That's a lot of dinners out, golf, tennis, trips to see the kids, or whatever you should be enjoying in retirement. In closing this chapter, I encourage you: *Don't ever let someone make you feel bad about doing what you believe is right for your money.*

Chapter 15 Market Accounts: Fee Based vs. Managed

"The first step to getting the things you want out of life is this: Decide what you want." **- Ben Stein**

"Zero is my hero in the market"

This could be one of the most published subjects in the financial world; however, it is also probably the most subjective. Trying to explain the whole system and how it works would be like someone trying to tell me on the telephone how to fly the Space Shuttle to the moon and back. It simply cannot be done. Everyone, including the "so-called" experts, has his or her own opinion on which market is the best, which stocks are best and why the markets go up and down. I'm going to explain to you my version of what is the purpose of the markets vs how they function.

What is the "market?" When most people think of the market, they are talking about the Dow Jones. The Dow Jones Industrial Average (DJIA), also called the Dow 30, is comprised of only 30 of the largest and most widely-held public companies in the United States. The Dow Jones is one of several stock market indices created by *The Wall Street Journal* editor and Dow Jones & Company co-founder Charles Dow. Why is the number 30 important? If a few of these stocks are not doing well, can that have a major effect on the overall return of this market? Yes! Since it is comprised of only 30 stocks, some argue that the DJIA is not a very accurate representation of the overall market performance, even though it is the most cited and most widely recognized of the stock market indices. Additionally, the DJIA is criticized for being a priceweighted average, giving relatively higher-priced stocks more influence over the average than their lower-priced counterparts.

Then you have the NASDAQ, made up of approximately 3,200 companies. The NASDAQ is the largest U.S. electronic stock market. It lists more companies on average and trades more shares per day than any other U.S. market. It is home to companies that are leaders across all areas of business including technology, retail, communications, financial services, transportation, media and biotechnology. With all the diversity within the NASDAQ, you can specifically segment where you are investing your money. Maybe good, maybe bad. One thing for certain is that you'd better keep up on every segment of the market where you are invested.

Next is the Standard and Poor's 500 (S&P 500). This is made up of 500 large-cap corporations, most U.S.-based. The index is the most notable of the many indices owned and maintained by Standard & Poor's, a division of McGraw-Hill. The S&P 500 is used in reference not only to the index but also to the 500 actual companies whose stocks are included in the index. All of the stocks in the index are those of large publicly held companies that trade on the two largest U.S. stock markets—The New York Stock Exchange and the NASDAQ. It is considered to be a bellwether for the US economy and a component of the Index of Leading Indicators. In my opinion, this may be more stable than the Dow, simply because of more diversity. The S&P 500 is widley used as an indicator of the broader market, since it includes both "growth" stocks (which inflated and then deflated in the dot-com bubble and bust) and generally less volatile "value" stocks. It also includes stocks from both the NASDAQ stock market and the NYSE. There are different categories of companies that comprise the various markets.

The market's purpose is to generate capital for business. Along the way it has become (or maybe always has been) the largest form of legalized gambling. Just think about it. You put money "down" or "in" a stock or fund with limited to no knowledge of the who, what, when, and how of each fund -- and then you hope for the best. If you're right, then you make money with unlimited potential. If you're wrong, you also have the chance of losing money with just as big of a downside. To me, that's gambling. So just like gambling in Las Vegas, we seek out the "odds-maker." These are people who watch everything on a day-to-day basis, if not minute-by-minute. They come up with the different classes of risk. RISK! A very big word we are going to touch more on later. A few of the different subclass categories: conservative, moderate, aggressive, high cap, large cap, income fund, etc… The list can go on and on, based on the company, but none is without RISK!

Risk and reward, as the saying goes. Some win, some lose, but the majority of Americans play the game. One of the things I find with most of my clients is that they have no idea of how much they have or how to figure out if they are facing risk. So I'm going to give you my easy version of how to discover your risk:

1. How old are you and when do you need or think you'll want to use this money?
2. Is this money taxable, tax deferred, or tax free?
3. Who is the money's beneficiary: You, your spouse, or children or grandchildren?
4. What percentage of this money are you willing to lose at any given moment— 10%, 50%, or all of it?
5. Are you retired or still working?
6. Did you earn this money or was it given to you?

IF THE ANSWERS TO THESE QUESTIONS LOOK LIKE THIS:

I'm 60 years old, the money is tax free, it's going to be handed down, I'm willing to lose it all, I'm retired, and I won it in the lottery. Then I say, "Go for it in the most aggressive accounts you can find." That has never happened to me. I find that no matter what the answers to these questions are, as people get older, they want to be more conservative. They just don't know how. They're stuck with what they have always done or they are still listening to a money manager who doesn't specifically work with seniors or older clients. Most brokerage managers are working with people of all ages; however, the majority are in the 30 to 60 age group, the working years. When you retire, your whole frame of mind changes when it comes to risk and growth. Some will deny that, but it's true.

Retirement is not about making money; it's about using the money you've made up to that point to last you the rest of your life. A recent study in AARP Magazine stated that the number one thing that senior retirees were afraid of is, "Am I going to outlive my money?" Number two was dying. So when I read that I came to this conclusion: You all (meaning seniors) would rather be dead than broke. That is what the survey says in a nutshell.

So why do people in retirement take so much risk in the market? My conclusion is simple; we get in a rut and continue to do the same thing as we always have, even when dramatic changes in life have taken place. More times than not, I'll be sitting down with a client for the first time and ask him, "Has anything changed in your life in the past year or two?" He will answer no. However, he just retired in the past six months. So I'll ask him what changes in his financial picture of income and risk has an advisor made. NONE is the most common answer. "He told me not to change a thing." Why is that? Is it for his benefit or yours? I think you probably already know.

This now brings me to a big question: How do I pay for the services on my account? When you have a brokerage account of any kind, costs will be involved. I think everyone can agree on that. But where do I get the biggest bang for my buck and what is fair? The answer can be totally subjective depending on whom you ask.

There are two basic types of brokerage accounts. First is the "managed" account. In this case, you put your money in an account with a firm or individual broker and he or she uses complete discretion to make any changes or trades at any time and as often as necessary. You don't pay any fee based on how much activity is on the account, rather you pay a one-time fee for the year, or possibly by the quarter, based on the whole amount of money in the account. Very commonly the rate is anywhere from about 1% to as high as 3%. Do the math and you'll find that if you have a $500,000 account at 1% per year, that is $5,000 win, lose or break even. The house is going to get this fee. This also may not include any service fees on the account, annual maintenance fees or other charges that can be present. This type of account can be a good deal if the following applies:

1. You have a very good broker managing your account either daily or weekly.
2. Your broker is making a lot of trades.
3. You want to be aggressive in the market.
4. You don't want to be involved.

These are just a few points to consider when choosing a managed account.

The second type of account is a "transactional" account. This means that you only pay a fee based on the number of times you or your broker decides to make a change to where your money is placed. You also may be subjected to all the other fees like maintenance fees, annual fees and any other nickel-and-dime changes. In transactional accounts usually you and your advisor have decided what investments you're comfortable with. You're going to periodically watch them to check their progress (or decline) and then make changes as needed. There are no annual fees involved; however, you're going to pay by the transaction. For example: You have 25 different stocks or mutual funds in your account and you've decided to move one to a different fund. You'll pay a fee based on either how much money is being moved or simply the transaction itself. Maybe $100 to as much as $500 per transaction. This is what you need to know going into this type of account: What are the transaction fees and how are they calculated–by the dollar amount being moved or by the number of shares?

In closing this section I'd like to say that both of these accounts can be viable ways to manage your money in a market account. However, you must know what you're willing to pay for the services and how involved you want to be in the active day-to-day management of the account. If you're like most people, you simply give your money to someone that you trust and hope for the best. Over the past few years, my biggest concern has been that, in talking with thousands of people, about 80% to 90% had no idea what type of account they had or what dollar figure they have been paying (SCARY!). Some of these folks have had accounts not only for years but decades with the same firm or broker.

Here is the best example I have of this: A couple from the Midwest had an account with a large national firm managed by a local representative. When I sat down with them the account had approximately $800,000 in it. They started the account with $400,000, 12 years before. I asked how the account had been doing and the response was "Well, that's why we're here." Not good. So as I'm looking through the account statement, I asked about the fees. His response was that he had been with this company so long that he had NO fees. To his surprise, I showed him on his statement that he was paying not only a management fee but also a transactional fee, totaling about 3% a year on the $800,000. He of course was thinking back over the past 11 years and trying to figure what he had really been paying. In reviewing the account statement for the past 11 years, which took some time, we determined that he had paid over $350,000 dollars in the past 12 years to his broker along with annual maintenance fees. If this had been a transactional fee account, because of the limited trades that they had made, he would only have paid $41,000 in fees for the exact same growth/losses each year. What we didn't figure in was the extra $309,000 that would be in his account and with interest accrued the balance should be $700,000 MORE. With the transactional-based account, his account would have been $1,500,000. Just a little different.

Which account is better? It depends on your goals, risk

tolerance, age and income needs. Just please ask questions and **KNOW WHAT YOU ARE PAYING**!

Chapter 16 How to Pick an Advisor or Estate Planner

Finding the right person can be a very, very difficult challenge. For many people, the task of finding a person is done simply by opening the phone book and throwing a dart. Guessing is not always the best way. Others simply accept on faith that their attorney is a qualified planner, when in fact most attorneys have little training or actual experience in this complex area. Still others will only shop price rather than the quality of the services provided. In most cases you'll want to find out how they are getting paid—from you or from the companies they represent? Not all services require you to pay directly from your dollars. I have found that attorneys all seem to require a fee for the legal part of your planning, and should. Legal services will always have a fee, but remember that you usually get what you pay for, so don't go to your general practitioner to have a will or trust drawn up. For example: If I come home to my wife and tell her that my left arm is numb and I'm having chest pains, I don't ask her to call my foot doctor. I would tell her to call the cardiologist—I'm having a heart attack. Not all attorneys provide the same services.

Estate planning involves the following: Legal work, financial planning, tax planning, and insurance and annuity planning. If you can find one person to do all of these things at the highest level of expertise, I surely don't know who that is. In most cases you're going to have your will or trust done by an attorney, your risk money by a broker, your taxes by your accountant, and your life insurance and long-term care needs by your insurance person or elder care planner. If you can find one person that will oversee all of this, great!

Here are a few simple questions to have answered before

moving forward with anyone:

- How long have you been doing this particular specialized planning?

- Are you licensed, and by whom?

- Are you part of a larger organization? (Or are you a "one-man show?")

- What kind of training are you required to have and how often do you have to take continuing education?

- What happens if you're no longer here as my planner? Who takes over the management of my affairs?

- Where can I check out your credentials?

- Do you have any references I can check?

After you have been educated on your particular needs, then and only then can you make a good decision for yourself. Get solid documentation on what you may be doing, and take your time. Unless, of course, you're in a crisis situation. Make sure you feel comfortable with all the surrounding circumstances before making a decision. Never let someone make you feel bad about doing what you feel is right with "Your Money."

Chapter 17 Where to Live in Retirement: The Transition from Independent Care to Assisted Care to Skilled Care

"I am still determined to be cheerful and happy in whatever situation I may be; for I have also learned from experience that the greater part of our happiness or misery depends upon our dispositions, and not upon our circumstances."- **Martha Washington**

There are five major areas to consider before making the decision on where to live after you retire. When I ask pre-retirees the question of where they may want to live in retirement, the most common first answer is, "Right here." All of my family is here, or I raised my family in this area, or I could never think of leaving my grandchildren. How quickly this thought process changes when the kids or grandchildren are possibly spread out all over the nation. Then and usually only then do they get to the next five areas: Lifestyle, housing and real estate, health care, weather and taxes.

Lifestyle

Your lifestyle is a very big factor to consider when you're trying to decide where to live in retirement. You may want to play golf and tennis daily, so living in the cold climate of the Colorado mountains probably isn't for you. Maybe you need or want to be in a setting where there are museums and galleries, so a remote area would not be suitable. Possibly you need to be close to transportation and airports for trips to see the kids and grandchildren. Your lifestyle plans for retirement should help you determine a location.

Housing and Real Estate

When you retire, housing is a big consideration. You may have to plan for an extended period of time and include health considerations, upkeep and maintenance at a minimum. Maybe you're looking for a condo or a retirement village that may have several choices of living accommodations. Today several types of retirement communities are considered to be full-service. For example, I visited a community in the Midwest that has apartments, assisted living, independent living, adult foster care housing, and a full skilled nursing facility all on the same community grounds. It had its own grocery stores, beauty salons, doctors offices, pharmacy, shops and even entertainment facilities for just about every activity imaginable. The most interesting thing about this community was that you paid only one flat rate per month no matter what level of care you needed or in which building you lived. You could move from independent living to skilled care and pay the same price. Some may say that you're paying too much for the services when you're completely independent, as opposed to getting a great deal for skilled care if ever needed. I guess the positive concept for most would be that you never again would have to be leaving your friends and relationships forged in your retirement years.

Health Care

We all understand that heathcare is one of the most important areas of consideration in retirement. If you have ongoing medical conditions, this will play a major role in your decision on where to live. You want to make sure that the proper facilities are available to serve your needs. Researching proper physician and medical outpatient facilities, as well as inpatient facilities, is crucial. If you are healthy, you may need to only consider the most basic health care needs, with more extensive services within close driving distances.

WEATHER

Weather and lifestyle go hand in hand. If your lifestyle dictates that you enjoy a lot of warm weather activities, then maybe Arizona or one of the Southern states is the best location. If you're a skier or hiker, then possibly one of the mountain states would fit better. Whatever your activities dictate, decide which climate you can tolerate and look for a retirement home in that geographic area.

TAXES

No matter where you live after retirement, you will have to pay some kind of taxes. Most states have an income tax but some do not tax retirement income or social security. There will be real estate taxes in almost all states; however, some have a homestead exemption that will lower the real estate tax for some older individuals. In addition, some states have a personal property tax that can be very costly if you have a lot of property subject to this particular tax. Other taxes to be considered are sales tax, county taxes, city taxes and so on. If you need to research the tax structure of any given state, you can simply go on that state's Website.

SENIORS BACK TO SCHOOL

A large number of seniors are choosing to live out their so-called "golden years" as vigorously as when they were in college. This may be spurred by the growing research suggesting that mental activity is a "fountain of youth." College-affiliated retirement communities have sprung up in at least 50 cities nationwide, linking retirees with notable schools such as Notre Dame, Cornell University, and Penn State, just to name a few.

These new communities have a wide variety of living

accommodations available, such as condominium developments, some with a community center on-site. Some of the others are continuing care facilities combining apartments with assisted living and nursing homes designed for people's changing needs as they age.

If you take the time to walk through a college campus today, you'll find that the demographic landscape is changing. Retirees and seniors are now in the mix with students, attending classes, and going to sporting and cultural events. According to *CNN Money*, many universities have responded to these changing demographics by creating academic courses and special pricing specifically for seniors. Senior educational programs are in more than 300 institutions nationwide.

According to *Consumer Reports*, other factors that also contribute to the growing interest in retirement in a college town include inexpensive food and entertainment, teaching hospitals and lower crime rates. Another important consideration is the opportunity to build intergenerational and diverse relationships and mentoring that benefit all generations.

Other Options

There is also a growing national demand for retirement housing for younger retirees, given that the first generation of Baby Boomers is now approaching their 60s and will soon retire. With the ever-growing population of younger retirees comes a desire for bigger and better amenities, such as social clubs and gyms. Retirees without the need for daily medical services or age-restricted developments are expanding nationwide and are not usually affiliated with a skilled nursing facility. According to a study done by the National Association of Home Builders, about 60 percent of such developments for those age 55 and older are now outside the Sun Belt, with the growth in northern states driven in part by many buyers' wishes to stay closer to their families and the communities where they spent their working lives.

No matter what your dream of retirement may encompass,

you should always address your concerns in order of importance. Make sure to consider your finances, including investment strategies and protection of your financial assets. Be sure to work with a qualified financial adviser who can help you create or update your personalized financial plan and integrate your short and long-term goals.

Chapter 18 Stories of Odd Places Where People Keep Their Money

Many people talk to me about where they keep their money. You might think when you're working with retirees or people over the age of 50, they would keep their money in financial vehicles such as stocks, bonds, mutual funds, CDs, or checking, savings, or money market accounts. The following are a few stories that I have heard over the years of where people have kept their money.

Story #1

I once worked with a couple whom I'll call Mr. & Mrs. Jones. At the first meeting we talked about possibly putting some of their money into different annuity products that seemed to fit their long-term goals. As I was sitting down with Mr. & Mrs. Jones, they said they had decided to put $50,000 into an annuity. Mr. Jones just needed to get the money for me, but wanted to start the paperwork that day. I proceeded to get out the paperwork, when Mr. Jones got up and left the room. A few minutes later he came back and set a utility knife down on the table. He knew I was confused by my puzzled expression, but he said to hold on one second. He picked up the utility knife, looked at a light switch on the wall, measured over about two feet, then took the knife and cut a hole in the wall. He pushed the dry wall in with his hand, reached down inside, and pulled out a bag with $50,000 in cash. He had sheetrocked it into the wall. Mr. Jones was a contractor, and said nobody would know where he hid this money except him or his wife. The money had been inside this wall for about five or six years. I told him to deposit it into the bank, so he could write a check for it.

Story # 2

This story was told by one of my agent advisors. Let's call him Rick. Rick was sitting down with a couple one evening, and the gentleman told him he didn't believe in banks. He didn't want to keep his money in a bank, so he kept different denominations of money at home. He also had some gold coins that he wanted to cash in and put into a financial product with us. Rick asked him if he kept them in a safety deposit box or a safe. The gentleman said he had it in a safe place. He actually had about $180,000 in gold coins in the gas tank of his tractor. He said no one was going to steal that damn old thing, and no one would ever know they were in there. Since the coins were down in the fuel, they weren't going to deteriorate or anything. He had to drain the gas tank, take the gold coins out to cash them in, and put the money into a financial product.

Story # 3

This happened to me one evening when I met with an 83-year-old gentleman and his 58-year-old son. I was sitting down with the son and the gentleman, whom I'll call Tom. Tom lived in a very small, worn house and drove an old, rusty truck. He didn't appear to have any kind of financial means. I had gone through a formula to figure out what his assets were, and he didn't really have any financial holdings. He said he was worried about what was going to happen to his retirement fund if he went into a nursing home. His son told Tom he really didn't have anything so he could qualify for Medicaid at any time. Tom argued that he was worried about his retirement funds, and said, "wait just a minute." He walked out into his bedroom. This was only a three-room house with the kitchen and dining room together, a little living area, bathroom and bedroom. There he pulled out a cardboard mail bin from his closet and returned to the kitchen where we were sitting. In this cardboard mail bin was a bunch of money in all denominations rolled up in balls and rubber banded together. The son's eyeballs almost popped out of his head.

He asked his dad where he had amassed all that money. Tom said he had saved it all those years, and this was his retirement fund. I asked how much money was in that mail bin, and he said $409,000. The son and I almost fell out of our chairs. Again, Tom said he was really worried about what would happen to this money if he went into a nursing home, or if the house burned down, but he just didn't believe in the bank system. So we started doing the paperwork to put this money into various financial products.

Tom took the bin and pushed it across the table to me. I said I was not taking it. I was in a very bad section of town, wearing a suit and a tie, and driving a fairly nice vehicle. Tom wanted me to take the huge mail bin filled with money out with me. I told him he should just paint a target on my back. I couldn't take that money. First, I wouldn't. Second, I shouldn't. And third, we needed to take it to a bank and put it into a cashier's check to send to the company. He said, "Oh no, son, my money doesn't go to the bank." I told him we were certainly not shipping it from Michigan to Texas where the insurance company was located.

I told Tom he could take that money and buy a new house or a new car, but he said, "No, that's my retirement." I asked him how old he was, and he said 83. I told him he should spend some of it, but the mentality was that he had saved and saved for a rainy day, and he didn't want to touch that money. I suggested we deliver it to my office and convert it to a cashier's check, knowing that it would go across the street to the bank. We called an armored car to have it picked up the next day.

No one ever knew about his money, and if that house would have burned down or if someone had robbed him, it would have been gone in an instant. Tom is still living in his little house and driving his beat up truck waiting for the "rainy day" to come. However, now his money is safe for him and his children, not to mention that it is also earning a great deal of interest.

Story # 4

I met with a couple who, like many folks, owned a home or had built a home next to the old farmhouse in which they grew up. Mom and dad lived in the farmhouse. The couple, Mr. and Mrs. Peters, were given an acre of land and built a home next to them. When the parents passed away, the couple sold the farmhouse to a young couple about 25 years of age. The old farmhouse was on one acre, and they sold it for $45,000. About five or six months passed by, and they called me to say they had come into some money and wanted to do some more investments. I asked them how much money they were looking to invest, and they said they had about $25,000. Since Mr. and Mrs. Peters had previously invested some money with me, I knew their entire portfolio. I kindly asked where it came from.

They said the young couple next door was putting up a fence in the back yard for their dog, and they found a box with money. In today's society I couldn't believe that the young couple even said anything about the box, but they did. They thought it must have belonged to the people who once lived there. They asked me what I thought they should do with that money, and I said that first, I would give some to the young couple who found that money. Second, I would dig up that whole backyard to see if there was more buried money, which they did. About three weeks later after the yard had been all dug up, they had found over $120,000 buried in the back yard. Some of it was so old that the money was silver certificates from back in the early 1900s. Today they are worth about double the face value. When it was all said and done, they paid off the house for the young couple, and they still had more than $50,000 left over.

I've learned that people bury money, and they put it in their

Bibles, walls or anywhere else. These stories are from people we call "Depression babies." They had either been through the Depression themselves, or heard their parents' stories of the Depression, and didn't trust banks. As a result, they hid money wherever they could stash it.

In my 10 years of meeting with people, I have found another interesting place where people keep their important documents: I could walk into someone's house and go right to the freezer, because 50% of the people over the age of 75 keep most of their important documents they don't want to burn, such as bonds, wills, and statements, in plastic baggies in the freezer. In many cases, they also keep cash there, which I don't recommend, but many people do. Today you can go to an office supply store and purchase a mini-safe or fireproof box to keep in your house.

Story # 5

This story, about another unusual place where clients keep their money, is from one of our advisor team members. Once he was meeting with a client and the gentleman said it was going to take him a few minutes to get his money, because he had about $15,000 to $20,000 in every toilet in the house. He had put twenty dollar bills in plastic baggies, and taped them to the inside of the toilet on the bottom where all the water collected in each of four bathrooms in his house. He now wanted to put that money in safer places, like investments. Needless to say, his life savings were saved from literally going down the toilet.

Story # 6

One day I was sitting in my former office in Lapeer, Michigan, when a lady walked in, and said she was becoming worried about what would happen to her money when she dies. I told her that one of the first things we like to know is if she has a will or a trust. She said no to both and told me that her husband died eight years ago. She went on to say that she didn't have any children.

She had outlived both of them, was 97 years old and was getting a little worried about what might happen to her money. I told her it was probably time she started to worry.

I next asked who would be her beneficiaries, and she said she wanted the money to go to her two grandchildren. Then I asked her approximately how much money she had. She said all of her money was in the bank. I asked where her money resided at the bank—in CD or savings. She said it was all in her checking account. I thought it probably wasn't much, because no one keeps a whole lot in a checking account.

When I asked how much was in her checking account, she said $2.1 million. I almost fell out of my chair, because, for one thing, it shouldn't be there, and for another thing, it shouldn't be there! I asked her how long it had been in her checking account, and she said about eight years. Since her husband died, she liquidated everything that they had in different investments, because she didn't understand them. I then asked if the bank told her to put that money in other areas. She said they wanted her to put it in a CD, but she was not even sure what that was, so she kept it in an account easy to access.

I asked how much interest her money was making in her checking account, and she said just a little over 1%. She said that the people at the bank just love me, and, of course, they would. The interest she had been giving up on her money, even calculated at 5%, had been paying the salaries of everyone in that bank for the past eight years.

However, I could not convince her to move her money into better areas that would earn her more interest. For her, it wasn't about making money, it was about setting up her estate plan so that upon her death her money would go directly to her heirs and not get tied up in probate.

The first recommendation I made to her grandchildren was that she needed to make a considerable donation to charity. They were shocked when I told them grandma should donate $200,000 to charity. Their first question was, "How much does grandma really have?" When they found out the amount, they too almost fell off their chairs.

Appendix A
ORGANIZATIONS

AARP
601 E Street, NW
Washington, DC 20049
800-424-3410
www.aarp.org

American Association of Homes and Services for the Aging (AAHSA)
2519 Connecticut Avenue, NW
Washington, DC 20008-1520
202-783-2242
www.aahsa.org

American Society on Aging
833 Market Street, Suite 512
San Francisco, CA 94103
415-882-2910
www.asaging.org

Assisted Living Federation of America (ALFA)
11200 Waples Mill Road
Fairfax, VA 22030
703-691-8100
www.alfa.org

The Centers for Medicare and Medicaid Services
7500 Security Boulevard
Baltimore, MD 21244
800 MEDICARE (633-4227)
www.medicare.gov

Clearinghouse on Abuse and Neglect of the Elderly (CANE)
University of Delaware
Department of Consumer Studies
Newark, DE 19716
302-831-3525
www.cane.udel.edu

Department of Health and Human Services
200 Independence Avenue, SW
Washington, DC 20201
877-696-6775
www.dhhs.gov

Department of Housing and
Urban Development (HUD)
HUD for Seniors
451 7th Street, SW
Washington, DC 20410
202-708-1112
www.hud.gov/groups/seniors.cfm

Department of Labor
Employment and Training Administration
Division of Older Worker Programs
200 Constitution Avenue, NW, Room N 4641
Washington, DC 20210
877-US2-JOBS
www.doleta.gov/seniors

Department of Veterans Affairs (VA)
810 Vermont Avenue, NW
Washington, DC 20420
800-827-1000
www.va.gov

Gerontological Society of America
1275 K Street, NW
Suite 350
Washington, DC 20005-4006
202-842-1275
www.geron.org

Meals on Wheels
1414 Prince Street, Suite 302
Alexandria, VA 22314
703-548-5558
www.mowaa.org

Medic Alert
2323 Colorado Avenue
Turlock, CA 95382
888-633-4298
www.medicalert.org

Medicare Beneficiaries Defense Fund
1460 Broadway
Eighth Floor
NewYork, NY 10036-7393
212-869-3850
www.medicarerights.org

National Academy of Elder Law Attorneys, Inc.
1604 North Country Club Road
Tucson, Arizona 85716
520-881-4005
www.naela.com

National Association of Area Agencies on Aging
927 15th Street NW, 6th Floor
Washington, DC 20005
202-296-8130
www.n4a.org

National Association for Home Care
228 7th Avenue Street, SE
Washington, DC 20003
202-547-7424
www.nahc.org

National Association for Hispanic Elderly
234 East Colorado Blvd
Pasadena, CA 91101
626-564-1988
www.anppm.org

National Association of Social Security Claimants Representatives
6 Prospect Street
Midland Park, NJ 07432-1691
800-431-2804
www.nosscr.org

National Association of State Units on Aging
1225 I Street, Suite 725
Washington, DC 20005
202-898-2578
www.nasua.org

National Caucus and Center on Black Aged, Inc.
1424 K Street, NW, Suite 500
Washington, DC 20005
202-637-8400
www.ncba-aged.org

National Center for Assisted Living
1201 L Street, NW
Washington, DC 20005
202-842-4444
www.ncal.org

National Center on Elder Abuse
1201 15th Street, NW
Suite 350
Washington, DC 20005
212-898-2586
www.ncea.aoa.gov

National Citizens' Coalition for Nursing Home Reform
1424 16th Street, NW, Suite 200
Washington, DC 20036-2211
202-332-2276
www.nccnhr.org

National Council on Aging
100 D Street, SW, Suite 801
Washington, DC 20024
202-479-1200
www.ncoa.org

National Funeral Director's Association
13625 Bishop's Drive
Brookfield, WI 53005-6607
414-541-2500
www.nfda.org

National Hispanic Council on Aging
2713 Ontario Road, NW
Washington, DC 20009
202-265-1288
www.nhcoa.org

National Hospice and Palliative Care Organization
1700 Diagonal Road, Suite 300
Alexandria, VA 22314
800-658-8898
www.nhpco.org

National Institute on Aging
Building 31, Room 5C27
31 Center Drive, MSC 2292
Bethesda, MD 20892
301-496-1752
www.nih.gov/nia

Long-Term Care Resource Center
Division of Health Services
University of Minnesota School of Public Health
420 Delaware Street, SE
Minneapolis, MN 55455
612-624-5171
www.hsr.umn.edu

National Network of Estate Planning Attorneys
410 17th Street, Suite 1260
Denver, CO 80202
800-638-8681
www.netplanning.com

National Senior Citizen Law Center
1815 H Street, NW, Suite 700
Washington, DC 20006
202-887-5280
www.nsclc.org

Office of Civil Rights
Federal Transit Administration
U.S. Department of Transportation
400 Seventh Street, SW, Room 9102
Washington, DC 20590
888-446-4511
www.fta.dot.gov

Office of Program Compliance and Disability Rights
Office of Fair Housing and Equal Opportunity
U.S. Department of Housing and Urban Development
451 7th Street, SW, Room 5242
Washington, DC 20410
202-708-1112
www.hud.gov/offices/fheo/index.cfm

Older Women's League
1750 NewYork Ave., NW
Suite 350
Washington, DC 20006
202-783-6686
www.owl-national.org

Senior Community Service Employment Program (SCSEP)
AARP National Office
601 E Street, NW
Washington DC 20049
202-434-2020
Locate a local office online at www.aarp.org/scseplocate

Social Security Administration
6401 Security Blvd
Baltimore, MD 21235
800-772-1213
www.ssa.gov

State Long-Term Care Insurance Partnerships
University of Maryland Center on Aging
1240 HHP Building
College Park, MD 20742
301-405-7555
www.inform.umd.edu/aging/PLTC/index.html

U.S. Department of Justice
Civil Rights Division
950 Pennsylvania Avenue, NW
Disability Rights Section- NYAV
Washington, DC 20530
800-514-0301
www.usdoj.gov/crt/ada/adahom1.htm

Visiting Nurses Association of America
11 Beacon Street, Suite 910
Boston, MA 02108
888-866-8773
www.vnaa.org

APPENDIX B
WEB SITES

DRIVING

AAA Foundation for Traffic Safety's Senior Web Site

www.seniordrivers.org

ELDERCARE

The AGS Foundation For Health In Aging

www.healthinaging.org

Eldercare Locator

www.eldercare.gov

EMPLOYMENT

Americans With Disabilities Act home page

www.usdoj.gov/crt/ada/adahom1.htm

AARP Best Employers for Seniors

www.aarp.org/bestemployers/

Benefits CheckUp

www.benefitscheckup.org

Senior Job Bank

www.seniorjobbank.com

GENERAL

Ageline Database

www.research.aarp.org/ageline/home.html

Americans With Disabilities Act home page

www.usdoj.gov/crt/ada/adahom1.htm

Benefits Checkup
www.benefitscheckup.org

Carrier Alert Program
www.nalc.org/commun/alert

Food Stamp Programs by State
www.cbpp.org/8-25-03fa.htm

National Council on Aging
www.ncoa.org

Senior Living
www.seniorliving.about.com

Senior Resource Directory
www.seniorresource.com

LEGAL

Americans with Disabilities Act
www.usdoj.gov/crt/ada/adahom1.htm

Elder Law Answers
www.elderlawanswers.com

USA Gov for Seniors
www.usa.gov/topics/seniors.shtml

Legal Aid Clinics
www.tcsg.org/lslinks.htm

MEDICARE/MEDICAID

Medicaid
www.cms.hhs.gov

Medicare
www.ssa.gov/mediinfo.htm

Medicare Participating Provider Physician Finder
www.medicare.gov/Physician/Home.asp

Medicare Participating Supplier finder
www.medicare.gov/Supplier/Home.asp

Medicare Personal Plan Finder
www.medicare.gov/MPPF/Home.asp

Medicare Publications and Information Sheets
www.medicare.gov

Medicare State Contacts
www.medicare.gov/contacts/home.asp

NURSING HOMES

Guide to Choosing a Nursing Home
www.healthfinder.gov/docs/doc00107.htm

Nursing Home Checklist
www.medicare.gov/nursing/checklist.asp

Nursing Home Inspection Reports and Comparisons
www.medicare.gov/Nursing/Overview.asp

Senior Living
www.seniorliving.about.com

Your Guide to Choosing a Nursing Home
www.medicare.gov/Publications/Pubs/pdf/nhguide.pdf

Appendix C
SENIOR LEGAL HOTLINE DIRECTORY

ARIZONA

Southern Arizona Legal Aid, Inc.
64 E. Broadway Blvd.
Tucson, AZ 85701
800-231-5441
520-623-5137

CALIFORNIA

Legal Services of Northern California
515 12th Street
Sacramento, CA 95814
800-222-1753
916-551-2140
www.seniorlegalhotline.org

CONNECTICUT

Connecticut Legal Services, Inc.
872 Main Street
PO Box 258
Willimantic, CT 06226
800-296-1467
www.ctelderlaw.org

DISTRICT OF COLUMBIA

Legal Counsel for the Elderly, AARP Foundation
601 E Street, NW
Washington, DC 20049
202-434-2170

GEORGIA

Georgia Senior Legal Hotline
2 Peachtree Street, Suite 9398
Atlanta, GA 30303
888-257-9519
404-657-9915
www.gabar.org/senhot.asp

HAWAII

Legal Aid Society of Hawaii
924 Bethel Street
Honolulu, HI 96813-5119
888-536-0011
808-536-0011
www.legalaidhawaii.org

IOWA

Legal Hotline for Older Iowans
1111 9th Street, Suite 230
Des Moines, IA 50314
800-992-8161
515-282-8161
www.iowalegalaid.org/hotline

IDAHO

Idaho Legal Aid Services
PO Box 913
310 North Fifth Street
Boise, ID 83701
866-345-0106
866-954-2591 (Spanish)
www.idaholegalaid.org

KANSAS

Kansas Legal Services
200 N. Broadway, Suite 500
Wichita, KS 67202
888-353-5337
316-265-9681
www.kansaslegalservices.org

KENTUCKY

Access to Justice Foundation
400 Old Vine Street, Suite 203
Lexington, KY 40507-1910
800-200-3633
www.accesstojustice.org

LOUISIANA

Southeast Louisiana Legal Services
1919 Common Street
New Orleans, LA 70112
504-529-1000
877-521-6242
www.nolac.org

MARYLAND

Legal Aid Bureau, Inc.
500 East Lexington Street
Baltimore, MD 21202
800-999-8904
410-539-5340
www.mdlab.org/srhotline.html

MAINE

Legal Services for the Elderly
9 Green Street
P.O. Box 2723
Augusta, ME 04338
800-750-5353
207-623-1797
www.mainelse.org

MICHIGAN

Elder Law Of Michigan, Inc.
222 N. Pine Street, Suite 720
Lansing, MI 48933
800-347-5297
517-372-5959
www.elderslaw.org

NEW HAMPSHIRE

New Hampshire Legal Assistance
1361 Elm Street
Manchester, NH 03101
888-353-9944
603-624-6000
www.nhla.org

NEW MEXICO

State Bar of New Mexico Special Projects, Inc.
P.O. Box 25883
Albuquerque, NM 87125
800-876-6657
505-797-6005
www.nmbar.org

NORTH DAKOTA

Legal Services of North Dakota
P.O. Box 1666
Minot, ND 58702-1666
866-621-9886
www.legalassist.org

OHIO

Pro Seniors' Legal Hotline
7162 Reading Road, Suite 1150
Cincinnati, OH 45237
800-488-6070
513-345-4160
www.proseniors.org

PENNSYLVANIA

Pennsylvania Senior Law HelpLine
100 South Broad Street
Philadelphia, PA 19110
877-727-7529
www.seniorlawcenter.org

SOUTH CAROLINA

South Carolina Centers for Equal Justice
1601K Shop Road
Columbia, SC 29201
888-346-5592
www.centersforequaljustice.org

TEXAS

Texas Legal Services Center
815 Brazos, Suite 1100
Austin, TX 78701
800-622-2520
www.tlsc.org/hotline.html

WASHINGTON

Northwest Justice Project
401 Second Avenue South, Suite 407
Seattle, WA 98104
888-387-7111
www.nwjustice.org

WEST VIRGINIA

West Virginia Senior Legal Aid
1988 Listravia Avenue
Morgantown, WV 26505
800-229-5068
304-291-3900
www.seniorlegalaid.org

WYOMING

Wyoming Legal Services
P.O. Box 1160
Lander, WY 82520
800-442-6710
307-332-6626

Appendix D
State-Specific Resources

	ALABAMA
Agency on Aging:	Alabama Dept. of Senior Services Montgomery, AL 36130 334-242-5743 www.aahha.org
Long-Term Care Ombudsman:	AL Dept. of Senior Services Montgomery, AL 36130 334-242-5743
Home/Hospice Care Organization:	Alabama Association of Home Health Agencies Montgomery, AL 36101 800-934-4312
Department of Public Health:	Alabama Department of Public Health www.alapubhealth.org
Elder Abuse Hotline Number:	800-458-7214
	ALASKA
Agency on Aging:	Alaska Commission on Aging Juneau, AK 99811 907-465-3250
Long-Term Care Ombudsman:	AK Mental Health Trust Auth. Anchorage, AK 99501 907-334-4480

Home/Hospice Care Organization:	Alaska Home Care Association Anchorage, AK 99518 907-565-6100
Elder Abuse Hotline Numbers:	800-478-9996 907-269-3666
	ARIZONA
Agency on Aging:	Aging and Adult Administration Phoenix, AZ 85007 602-542-4446
Long-Term Care Ombudsman:	AZ Aging & Adult Administration Phoenix, AZ 85007 602-542-6454
Home/Hospice Care Organization:	Arizona Association for Home Care Tempe, AZ 85282 480-967-2624
Department of Public Health:	Arizona Dept. of Health Services www.hs.state.az.us
Elder Abuse Hotline Number:	877-767-2385
	ARKANSAS
Agency on Aging:	Division Aging and Adult Services Little Rock, AR 72203 501-682-2441
Long-Term Care Ombudsman:	AR Division of Aging & Adult Services Little Rock, AR 72201-1437 501-682-8952

Home/Hospice Care Organization:	Home Care Association of AR Little Rock, AR 72201 501-682-8952
Department of Public Health:	Arkansas Dept. of Health http://hea1thyarkansas.com
Elder Abuse Hotline Numbers:	800-482-8049 800-582-4887
	CALIFORNIA
Agency on Aging:	California Department of Aging Sacramento, CA 95814 916-322-5290
Long-Term Care Ombudsman:	CA Department on Aging Sacramento, CA 95814 916-322-3887
Home/Hospice Care Organization:	California Association for Health Servicesat Home Sacramento, CA 95814 916-443-8055
Department. of Public Health:	California Department of Health Services www.dhs.cahwnet.gov
Elder Abuse Hotline Numbers:	888-436-3600 800-231-4024
	COLORADO
Agency on Aging:	Aging and Adult Services Denver, CO 80203 303-866-2800

Long-Term Care Ombudsman:	The Legal Center Denver, CO 80203 800-288-1376
Home/Hospice Care Organization:	Home Care Association of Colorado Englewood, CO 80112 303-694-4728
Department of Public Health:	Colorado Department of Public Health and Environment: www.state.co.us/gov_dir/cdphe_dir
Elder Abuse Hotline Numbers:	800-773-1366 800-866-7689
	CONNECTICUT
Agency on Aging:	Division of Elderly Services Hartford, CT 06106-5033 860-424-5298
Long-Term Care Ombudsman:	CT Department of Social Services Hartford, CT 06106 860-424-5200
Home/Hospice Care Organization:	Connecticut Association for Home Care, Inc. Wallingford, CT 06492 203-265-9931
Department of Public Health:	Connecticut Department of Health: www.state.ct.us/dph
Elder Abuse Hotline Numbers:	888-385-4225 860-424-5241

DELAWARE

Agency on Aging:	Delaware Division of Services for Aging and Adults with Physical Disabilities New Castle, DE 19720 302-577-4791
Long-Term Care Ombudsman:	Division of Services for Aging & Adults New Castle, DE 19720 302-577-4791
Home/Hospice Care Organization:	Home Health Corp of America Newark, DE 19711 800-333-4208
	Delaware Hospice Association Wilmington, DE 19810
Elder Abuse Hotline Numbers:	800-838-9800 800-223-9074

DISTRICT OF COLUMBIA

Agency on Aging:	District of Columbia Office on Aging Washington, DC 20001 202-724-5622
Long-Term Care Ombudsman:	Legal Counsel for the Elderly Washington, DC 20049 202-434-2140
Home/Hospice Care Organization:	MarylandNational Capital Homecare Assn Alexandria, VA 22314 708-535-1885
Elder Abuse Hotline Numbers:	202-541-3950 202-434-2140

FLORIDA

Agency on Aging:	Department of Elder Affairs Tallahassee, FL 32399 850-414-2000
Long-Term Care Ombudsman:	Florida State LTC Ombudsman Council Tallahassee, FL 32301 888-831–0404
Home/Hospice Care Organization:	Associated Home Health Industries of Florida, Inc. Tallahassee, FL 32301-2600 850-222-8967
	Florida Hospital Association Orlando, FL 32803 407-841–6230
Department of Public Health:	Florida Department of Health www.doh.state.fl.us
Elder Abuse Hotline Number:	800-962-2873

GEORGIA

Agency on Aging:	Division of Aging Services Atlanta, GA 30303 404-657-5258
Long-Term Care Ombudsman:	Office of the State LTCO Atlanta, GA 30303-3142 888-454-5826

Home/Hospice Care Organization:	Georgia Association for Comprehensive Home Care, Inc. Marietta, GA 30062 770-565-4531
Department of Public Health:	Georgia Division of Public Health: www.ph.dhr.state.ga.us
Elder Abuse Hotline Numbers:	404-657-5726 404-657-4076

HAWAII

Agency on Aging:	Hawaii Executive Office on Aging Honolulu, HI 96813 808-586-0100
Long-Term Care Ombudsman:	Executive Office on Aging Honolulu, HI 96813 808-586-0100
Home/Hospice Care Organization:	Home Care and Hospice Division, Healthcare Association of Hawaii Honolulu, HI 96814 808-521–8961
Department of Public Health:	Hawaii Department of Health www.hawaii.gov/health
Elder Abuse Hotline Numbers:	808-832-5115 (Oahu) 808-243-5151 (Maui) 808-241-3432 (Kauai) 808-933-8820 (East Hawaii) 808-327-6280 (West Hawaii)

	IDAHO
Agency on Aging:	Idaho Commission on Aging Boise, ID 83720-0007 208-334-3833
Long-Term Care Ombudsman:	Idaho Commission on Aging Boise, ID 83720 208-334-2220
Home/Hospice Care Organization:	Idaho Association of Home Health Agencies Boise, ID 83707 208-362-8190
Department of Public Health:	Idaho Department of Health and Welfare www.state.id.us/dhw/hwgd_www/home.html
Elder Abuse Hotline Numbers:	208-334-3833 208-364-1899
	ILLINOIS
Agency on Aging:	Illinois Department on Aging Springfield, IL 62701-1789 217-785-3356 Chicago Office: 312-814-2630 Instate toll free Senior HelpLine: 800-252-8966
Long-Term Care Ombudsman:	Illinois Department on Aging Springfield, IL 62701 217-785-3143

Home/Hospice Care Organization:	Illinois Home Care Council Glenview, IL 60025 847-657-6960 VNA First LaGrange, IL 60525 7087882047
Department of Public Health:	Illinois Department of Public Health: www.idph.state.il.us
Elder Abuse Hotline Numbers:	800-252-8966 800-252-4343
	INDIANA
Agency on Aging:	Bureau of Aging and InHome Services Indianapolis, IN 46207-7083 317-232-7020
Long-Term Care Ombudsman:	Indiana Division Disabilities Rehab Services Indianapolis, IN 46207 800-545-7763
Home/Hospice Care Organization:	Indiana Association for Home and Hospice Care, Inc. Indianapolis, IN 46250 317-844-6630
Department of Public Health:	Indiana State Department of Health www.in.gov/isdh
Elder Abuse Hotline Number:	800-992-6978

IOWA

Agency on Aging:	Iowa Department of Elder Affairs Des Moines, IA 50309-3609 515-242-3333
Long-Term Care Ombudsman:	Iowa Department of Elder Affairs Des Moines, IA 50309 515-242-3327
Home/Hospice Care Organization:	Iowa Association for Home Care Des Moines, IA 50309 515-282-3965
	Iowa Hospice Organization Des Moines, IA 50309 515-243-1046
Department of Public Health:	Iowa Department of Health http://idph.state.ia.us
Elder Abuse Hotline Numbers:	800-362-2178 515-281-4115

KANSAS

Agency on Aging:	Department on Aging Topeka, KS 66603 785-296-4986
Long-Term Care Ombudsman:	Kansas Office of the State LTC Ombudsman Topeka, KS 66612 785-296-3017

Home/Hospice Care Organization:	Kansas Home Care Association Lawrence, KS 66047 785-841-8611
	Association of Kansas Hospice Witchita, KS 67213 316-263-6380
Department of Public Health:	Kansas Department of Health and Environment www.ink.org/public/kdhe
Elder Abuse Hotline Numbers:	800-922-5330 785-296-0044 800-842-0078

KENTUCKY

Agency on Aging:	Office of Aging Services Frankfort, KY 40621 502-564-6930
Long-Term Care Ombudsman:	Office of Aging Services Frankfort, KY 40621 502-564-6930
Home/Hospice Care Organization:	Kentucky Home Health Association Lexington, KY 40517 859-268-2574
Elder Abuse Hotline Numbers:	800-752-6200 800-372-2991

LOUISIANA

Agency on Aging:	Governor's Office of Elderly Affairs Baton Rouge, LA 70898 225-342-7100
Long-Term Care Ombudsman:	Office of Elderly Affairs Baton Rouge, LA 70898 225-342-7100
Home/Hospice Care Organization:	HomeCare Association of Louisiana New Iberia, LA 70562 337-560-9610
Elder Abuse Hotline Number:	800-259-4990

MAINE

Agency on Aging:	Bureau of Elder and Adult Services Augusta, ME 04333 207-624-5335
Long-Term Care Ombudsman:	Maine LTC Ombudsman Program Augusta, ME 04332 207-621-1079
Home/Hospice Care Organization:	Home Care Alliance of Maine Augusta, ME 04330 207-623-0345
Elder Abuse Hotline Number:	800-624-8404

MARYLAND

Agency on Aging:	Maryland Department of Aging Baltimore, MD 21201-2374 410-767-1100
Long-Term Care Ombudsman:	Maryland Department of Aging Baltimore, MD 21201 410-767-1100
Home/Hospice Care Organization:	Maryland National Capital Homecare Association Alexandria,VA 22314 703-535-1885
Department of Public Health:	Maryland Department of Health and Mental Hygiene www.mdpublichealth.org
Elder Abuse Hotline Number:	800-917-7383

MASSACHUSE1TS

Agency on Aging:	Massachusetts Executive Office of Elder Affairs Boston, MA 02108 617-727-7750
Long-Term Care Ombudsman:	Massachusetts Executive Office of Elder Affairs Boston, MA 02108 617-727-7750

Home/Hospice Care Organization:	Massachusetts Council for Home Care Aide Services Boston, MA 02114 617-227-6641
	Visiting Nurses Association of New England Needham, MA 02194 781-444-0713
Department of Public Health:	Massachusetts Department of Health www.magnet.state.ma.us/dph/dphhome.htm
Elder Abuse Hotline Numbers:	800-922-2275 800-462-5540

MICHIGAN

Agency on Aging:	Michigan Office of Services to the Aging Lansing, MI 48909 517-373-8230
Long-Term Care Ombudsman:	Elderlaw of Michigan Lansing, MI 48933 866-485-9393
Home/Hospice Care Organization:	Michigan Home Health Association Okemos, MI 48864 517-349-8089
Department of Public Health:	Michigan Department of Public Health www.mdch.state.mi.us
Elder Abuse Hotline Numbers:	800-996-6228 800-882-6006

MINNESOTA

Agency on Aging:	Minnesota Board on Aging St. Paul, MN 55155-3843 651-296-2770
Long-Term Care Ombudsman:	Office of Ombudsman for Older Minnesotans St. Paul, MN 55101 800-657-3591
Home/Hospice Care Organization:	Minnesota HomeCare Association St. Paul, MN 55113-4036 651-635-0607
Department of Public Health:	Minnesota Department of Public Health www.health.state.mn.us
Elder Abuse Hotline Number:	800-333-2433

MISSISSIPPI

Agency on Aging:	Division of Aging and Adult Services Jackson, MS 39202 601-359-4925
Long-Term Care Ombudsman:	MS Department of Human Services, Div. of Aging Jackson, MS 39202 601-359-4927
Home/Hospice Care Organization:	Mississippi Association for Home Care Ridgeland, MS 39158 601-853-7533

	Mississippi Hospital Association Jackson, MS 39236 601-368-3220
Department of Public Health:	Mississippi Department of Health www.msdh.state.ms.us
Elder Abuse Hotline Numbers:	800-222-8000 800-227-7308
	MISSOURI
Agency on Aging:	Division on Aging Jefferson City, MO 65102 573-751-3082
Long-Term Care Ombudsman:	Department of Health & Senior Services Jefferson City, MO 65102 800-309-3282
Home/Hospice Care Organization:	Missouri Alliance for Home Care Jefferson City, MO 65109 573-634-7772
	Missouri Hospital Home Health Council Jefferson City, MO 65102 573-893-3700
Department of Public Health:	Missouri Department of Health www.health.state.mo.us
Elder Abuse Hotline Number:	800-392-0210

MONTANA

Agency on Aging:	Senior and Long Term Care Division Helena, MT 59620 406-444-4077
Long-Term Care Ombudsman:	Montana Department of Health & Human Services Helena, MT 59604 406-444-4676
Home/Hospice Care Organization:	Montana Association of Home Health Agencies Missoula, MT 59801 406-721-4035
	Montana Hospital Association Helena, MT 59604 406-442-1911
Department of Public Health:	Montana Department of Health www.mt.gov
Elder Abuse Hotline Number:	800-332-2272

NEBRASKA

Agency on Aging:	Division on Aging Lincoln, NE 68509 402-471-2307
Long-Term Care Ombudsman:	Division of Aging Services Lincoln, NE 68509 402-471-2307

Home/Hospice Care Organization:	Nebraska Association of Home and Community Health Agencies Lincoln, NE 68516 402-489-1117
Department of Public Health:	Nebraska Department of Health www.hhs.state.ne.us
Elder Abuse Hotline Number:	800-652-1999

NEVADA

Agency on Aging:	Nevada Division for Aging Services Carson City, NV 89706 775-687-4210
Long-Term Care Ombudsman:	Nevada Division for Aging Services Reno, NV 89502 775-688-2964
Home/Hospice Care Organization:	Home Health Care Assn of Nevada Reno, NV 89502 775-982-5860
Elder Abuse Hotline Numbers:	800-992-5757 702-784-8090 (Reno area)

NEW HAMPSHIRE

Agency on Aging:	Division of Elderly and Adult Services Concord, NH 03301 603-271-4680
Long-Term Care Ombudsman:	NH LTC Ombudsman Program Concord, NH 03301 603-271-4375

Home/Hospice Care Organization:	Home Care Association of New Hampshire Concord, NH 03301 603-225-5597
Department of Public Health:	New Hampshire Department of Health and Human Services www.dhhs.state.nh.us/Index.nsf?open
Elder Abuse Hotline Numbers:	800-949-0470 603-271-4386 800-442-5640

NEW JERSEY

Agency on Aging:	Department of Health and Senior Services Trenton, NJ 08625-0807 609-943-3436 800-792-8820
Long-Term Care Ombudsman:	Office of Ombudsman for Institutional Elderly Trenton, NJ 08625 609-943-4026
Home/Hospice Care Organization:	Home Health Assembly of New Jersey, Inc. Princeton Junction, NJ 08550 609-275-6100
	Home Care Council of New Jersey Verona, NJ 07044 973-857-3333

	New Jersey Hospital Association Princeton, NJ 08543 609-275-4000
Department of Public Health:	New Jersey Department of Health and Senior Services www.state.nj.us/health
Elder Abuse Hotline Number:	800-792-8820
	NEW MEXICO
Agency on Aging:	State Agency on Aging Santa Fe, NM 87501 505-827-7640
Long-Term Care Ombudsman:	State LTC Ombudsman Albuquerque, NM 87110 505-255-0971
Home/Hospice Care Organization:	New Mexico Association for Home Care Albuquerque, NM 87110 505-889-4556
Department of Public Health:	New Mexico Department of Health www.health.state.nm.us/website.nsf/frames?readform
Elder Abuse Hotline Numbers:	800-797-3260 505-841-6100
	NEW YORK
Agency on Aging:	New York State Office for the Aging Albany, NY 12223 800-342-9871

Long-Term Care Ombudsman:	New York State Office for the Aging Albany, NY 12223 518-474-7329
Home/Hospice Care Organization:	Home Care Association of New York State, Inc. Albany, NY 12210 518-426-8764
	New York State Association of Health Care Providers, Inc. Albany, NY 12207 518-463-1118
	Health Care Association of New York State Rensselaer, NY 12144 518-431-7600
	Hospice and Palliative Care Assn of New York State Albany, NY 12205 518-446-1483
	Home Care Council of New York City New York, NY 10036 646-366-0860
Department of Public Health:	New York State Department of Health www.health.state.ny.us
Elder Abuse Hotline Numbers:	800-342-9871 800-220-7184 (N. Eastern) 800-425-0314 (Buffalo) 800-837-9018 (Rochester)

800-425-0319 (Syracuse)
800-425-0316 (New York City)
800-425-0320 (L. Hudson Vly)
800-425-0323 (Long Island)

NORTH CAROLINA

Agency on Aging:	Department of Health and Human Services Raleigh, NC 27699 919-733-3983
Long-Term Care Ombudsman:	North Carolina Division of Aging Raleigh, NC 27699 919-733-8395
Home/Hospice Care Organization:	Association for Home Care and Hospice of North Carolina, Inc. Raleigh, NC 27609 919-848-3450
	The Carolinas Center for Hospice and End of Life Care Raleigh, NC 27609 919-878-1717
Department of Public Health:	North Carolina Department of Public Health www.dhhs.state.nc.us
Elder Abuse Hotline Number:	800-662-7030

NORTH DAKOTA

Agency on Aging:
Department of Human Services
Aging Services Division
Bismarck, ND 58504
800-451-8693

Long-Term Care Ombudsman:
Aging Services Division
Bismarck, ND 58504
800-451–8693

Home/Hospice Care Organization:
North Dakota Association for Home Care
Bismarck, ND 58502
701-224-1815

Department of Public Health:
North Dakota Department of Health
www.ehs.health.state.nd.us/ndhd

Elder Abuse Hotline Number:
800-451-8693

OHIO

Agency on Aging:
Ohio Department of Aging
Columbus, OH 43215-5928
614-466-5500

Long-Term Care Ombudsman:
Ohio Department of Aging
Columbus, OH 43215
614-466-1221

Home/Hospice Care Organization:
Ohio Council for Home Care
Columbus, OH 43229
614-885-0434

	Ohio Hospice & Palliative Care Organization Columbus, OH 43221 614-485-0021
Department of Public Health:	Ohio Department of Health www.odh.state.oh.us
Elder Abuse Hotline Numbers:	800-635-3748 800-282-1206
	OKLAHOMA
Agency on Aging:	Aging Services Division Oklahoma City, OK 73125 405-521-2281 or 521-2327
Long-Term Care Ombudsman:	Aging Services Division OK Department Oklahoma City, OK 73105 405-521-6734
Home/Hospice Care Organization:	Oklahoma Association for Home Care Oklahoma City, OK 73127 405-495-5995
Department of Public Health:	Oklahoma State Department of Health www.health.state.ok.us
Elder Abuse Hotline Number:	800-522-3511
	OREGON
Agency on Aging:	Senior and Disabled Services Division Salem, OR 97301 503-945-5811

Long-Term Care Ombudsman:	Oregon Office of the LTC Ombudsman Salem, OR 97305 503-378-6533
Home/Hospice Care Organization:	Oregon Association for Home Care Salem, OR 97302 503-364-2733
Department of Public Health:	Oregon Department of Human Resources www.ohd.hr.state.or.us
Elder Abuse Hotline Number:	800-232-3020
	PENNSYLVANIA
Agency on Aging:	Pennsylvania Department of Aging Harrisburg, PA 17101 717-783-1550
Long-Term Care Ombudsman:	Pennsylvania Department of Aging Harrisburg, PA 17101 717-783-7247
Home/Hospice Care Organization:	Pennsylvania Homecare Association Lemoyne, PA 17043 717-975-9448
Department of Public Health:	Pennsylvania Department of Health http://webserver.health.state.pa.us/health/site
Elder Abuse Hotline Numbers:	800-490-8505 800-254-5164

PUERTO RICO

Agency on Aging:	Governor's Office of Elderly Affairs Old San Juan Station, PR 00902 787-721-5710
Long-Term Care Ombudsman:	Puerto Rico Governor's Office Elder Affairs San Juan, PR 00902 787-725-1515
Home/Hospice Care Organization:	Puerto Rico Home Health Agencies and Hospices Association Arecibo, PR 00614 787-879-2955
Elder Abuse Hotline Numbers:	787-725-9788 787-721-8225

RHODE ISLAND

Agency on Aging:	Department of Elderly Affairs Providence, RI 02903 401-222-2858
Long-Term Care Ombudsman:	Alliance for Better Long Term Care Warwick, RI 02888 401-785-3340
Home/Hospice Care Organization:	Rhode Island Partnership for Home Care, Inc. Providence, RI 02906 401-751-2487

Department of Public Health:	Rhode Island Department of Health www.health.state.ri.us
Elder Abuse Hotline Numbers:	401-462-0550 401-785-3340

SOUTH CAROLINA

Agency on Aging:	Office of Senior and Long Term Care Services Columbia, SC 29202 803-898-2501
Long-Term Care Ombudsman:	SC DHHS, Office Aging Columbia, SC 29202 803-898-2850
Home/Hospice Care Organization:	South Carolina Home Care Association Columbia, SC 29202 803-254-7355
	Hospice for the Carolinas West Columbia, SC 29171-6009 803-791-4220
Department of Public Health:	South Carolina Department of Health and Environmental Control www.state.sc.us:80/dhec
Elder Abuse Hotline Numbers:	800-898-7318 800-898-2850

SOUTH DAKOTA

Agency on Aging:	Office of Adult Services and Aging Pierre, SD 57501 605-773-3656
Long-Term Care Ombudsman:	SD Office of Adult Services & Aging Pierre, SD 57501 605-773-3656
Home/Hospice Care Organization:	South Dakota Association of Healthcare Organizations Sioux Falls, SD 57106 605-361-2281
Department of Public Health:	South Dakota Department of Health www.state.sd.us/state/executive/doh/doh.html
Elder Abuse Hotline Number:	605-773-3656

TENNESSEE

Agency on Aging:	Commission on Aging and Disability Nashville, TN 37243 615-741-2056
Long-Term Care Ombudsman:	TN Commission on Aging and Disability Nashville, TN 37243 615-741-2056
Home/Hospice Care Organization:	Tennessee Association for Home Care, Inc. Nashville, TN 37214 615-885-3399

	Tennessee Hospital Association Home Care Alliance Nashville, TN 37210 615-256-8240
Department of Public Health:	Tennessee Department of Health www.state.tn.us/health
Elder Abuse Hotline Number:	888-277-8366

TEXAS

Agency on Aging:	Texas Department on Aging Austin, TX 78751 512-424-6840
Long-Term Care Ombudsman:	Texas Department on Aging Austin, TX 78711 512-424-6875
Home/Hospice Care Organization:	Texas Association for Home Care 3737 Executive Center Drive Austin, TX 78731 512-338-9293
Department of Public Health:	Texas Department of Health www.tdh.texas.gov
Elder Abuse Hotline Numbers:	512-834-3784 800-252-5400 512-438-2633 800-458-9858

UTAH

Agency on Aging:	Division of Aging & Adult Services Salt Lake City, UT 84145 801-538-3910
Long-Term Care Ombudsman:	Utah Division of Aging & Adult Services Salt Lake City, UT 84103 801-538-3924
Home/Hospice Care Organization:	Utah Association of Home Health Agencies Midvale, UT 84047 801-255-5888
Department of Public Health:	Utah Department of Health http://hlunix.ex.state.ut.us
Elder Abuse Hotline Numbers:	801-264-7669 800-371-7897

VERMONT

Agency on Aging:	Vermont Department of Aging and Disabilities Waterbury, VT 05671 802-241-2400
Long-Term Care Ombudsman:	Vermont Legal Aid, Inc. Burlington, VT 05402 802-863-5620
Home/Hospice Care Organization:	Vermont Assembly of Home Health Agencies Montpelier, VT 05602 802-229-0579

Elder Abuse Hotline Number:	800-564-1612

	VIRGINIA
Agency on Aging:	Virginia Department for the Aging Richmond, VA 23229 804-662-9333
Long-Term Care Ombudsman:	Virginia Association Area Agencies on Aging Richmond, VA 23219 804-644-2804
Home/Hospice Care Organization:	Virginia Association for Home Care Richmond, VA 23226 800-755-8636
	Virginia Hospital and Health Care Association Richmond, VA 23294 804-965-1249
Department of Public Health:	Virginia Department of Health www.vdh.state.va.us
Elder Abuse Hotline Numbers:	888-832-3858 804-371-0896

	WASHINGTON
Agency on Aging:	Aging and Adult Services Administration Olympia, WA 98504 360-725-2310 Instate only: 800-422-3263

Long-Term Care Ombudsman:	South King County MultiService Center Federal Way, WA 98093 253-838-6810
Home/Hospice Care Organization:	Home Care Association of Washington Edmonds, WA 98020 425-775-8120
Department of Public Health:	Washington State Department of Health www.doh.wa.gov
Elder Abuse Hotline Numbers:	800-422-3263 800-562-6078
	WEST VIRGINIA
Agency on Aging:	West Virginia Bureau of Senior Services Charleston, WV 25305 304-558-3317
Long-Term Care Ombudsman:	West Virginia Bureau of Senior Services Charleston, WV 25302 304-558-3317
Home/Hospice Care Organization:	West Virginia Council of Home Care Agencies, Inc. Middlebourne, WV 26149 304-758-4312
Elder Abuse Hotline Number:	800-352-6513

WISCONSIN

Agency on Aging:	Bureau of Aging and Long Term Care Resources Madison, WI 53707 608-266-2536
Long-Term Care Ombudsman:	Wisconsin Board on Aging & Long Term Care Madison, WI 53703 608-266-8945
Home/Hospice Care Organization:	Wisconsin Homecare Organization Madison, WI 53719 608-278-1115
Department of Public Health:	Wisconsin Department of Health and Family Services www.dhfs.state.wi.us
Elder Abuse Hotline Numbers:	608-266-2536 800-815-0015 608-246-7013

WYOMING

Agency on Aging:	Division on Aging Cheyenne, WY 82002 307-777-7986
Long-Term Care Ombudsman:	Wyoming Senior Citizens, Inc Wheatland, WY 82201 307-322-5553

Home/Hospice Care Organization:	Home Health Care Alliance of Wyoming Casper, WY 82601 307-237-7042
Department of Public Health:	Wyoming Department of Health http://wdhfs.state.wy.us/WDH
Elder Abuse Hotline Numbers:	307-777-6137 307-777-7123